# SATURDAY

THE WORDS I WROTE WHILE WAITING ON JESUS

# NOTHING

TO: BRADEN!

# SATURDAY

THE WORDS I WROTE WHILE WAITING ON JESUS

# NOTHING

*Josh Martin* (signature)

A MEMOIR BY

## JOSH MARTIN

THANKS!

Content Editing: Timothy Travaglini
Cover Design: Joey Seales (goodsouldesign.com)
Website: Brian Kalwat (briankalwat.com)

*Mom,*

*I wrote this because you let me live it. Thanks for giving me grace to leave, and learn, and even live in a car for a while. I wish everyone who reads this could meet you. I'm sure they would adore you as much as I do.*

THE PRELUDE //

*Jesus the Christ died on Friday, rose on Sunday,*
*and left the world to wonder on a Saturday filled with nothing.*

# THE PRELUDE

## the nothing day

It was the most agonizing day in human history. Picture hundreds of men and women lying in bed battling tears, staring at their ceiling, wishing the day before was all a bad dream. Husbands held their wives in silence, disciples dragged themselves through despair, children asked why. Fog filled the air and the heart. The pain felt personal, even more than it should. It was as though every follower of Jesus not only witnessed His death, but somehow, in some way, died with Him.

Jesus wasn't ordinary. While He was alive, wherever He went, His reputation beat Him there. He told provocative stories. He spoke of justice and equality and a future rescue. Healing seemed to live in His hands—authority released with His words. People drew near to Jesus with expectation, and He wasn't one to disappoint. In His presence was promise. Even the skeptic wondered if He was the long awaited King— the rumored Messiah. But now, in an instant, He was gone—crucified by the corrupt system He had been alleged to overthrow.

Messiah talk gave a discouraged people reason to dream again, but their grandest dreams were buried with Jesus. Eternity invaded earth when Jesus was born, but hell invaded heaven when He died. Or so it seemed.

In many ears though, an echo of a Voice still spoke. In many hearts, a flicker of Light still shone. But the unknown, the terrible unknown—the waiting, the nothing, the gray sky overhead—can become unbearable, even in the most faithful heart.

For the first century believer, the waiting lasted a day. Jesus was killed on Friday, Saturday nothing, but Sunday, bewildering Sunday, the tomb was empty, the promise come.

For the twenty-first century believer, the story is much the same. We live in the day between—the nothing day. Our lives unfold somewhere between the blessed resurrection and the promised second coming. The promise is promised but has not yet come. Fulfillment is both far and near.

We live in the meantime—the mysterious place of in-between. The Kingdom of God has come, is among us now, available to us, yet somehow still coming one day to fully liberate. We are married and engaged—betrothed and consummated—born and to be born—healed and healing—so tangibly near, so untouchably far. We are preparing for a wedding in which the vows have already been spoken, the kiss already given. Our covenant and God are old, new, here, there, now, forever, and yet, somehow, still to come.

The trouble of our Saturday is it lasts longer than a day.

Our waiting, trusting, and nothing could very well last a lifetime. In our minds and hearts there is hope that cannot be explained away—truth that will not be shaken—but still in our minds and hearts we battle doubt, anxiety, questions, pain, suffering, and mystery.

The human soul has a love/hate relationship with mystery. We are afraid of mystery—intrigued by mystery. We cover our eyes with our hands, say we do not wish to look, certainly we cannot bear to see, all the while cracking our fingers hoping to catch a glimpse.

Extreme fear and irresistible interest live in Saturday.

After Jesus defeated death and left the tomb, the first thing He did was visit His followers. He found them together in an upper room, and in that room, among those people, was great faith, great confusion, great anxiety, great fear, great longing. They were a transcendent community. No one would have ever been asked to leave because they confessed worry or doubt. The first followers of Jesus, who were together that first Sunday, were not perfect, not likely patient, not cultured or refined, but in a very basic sense, they were being healed because they were present.

In the meantime, in the in-between, they gathered, prayed, and hoped recklessly. They sat with each other. For a day and a half, they sat with each other. They looked across the room with blank stares. They bit their fingernails. They paced. They tried to eat but couldn't. They had a hard time breathing. They fainted in exhaustion. They embraced the emotion—because embracing the emotion is essential to the process.

Many of the people in that room on Saturday and historic Sunday were responsible for the expansion and leading of the early church. And Jesus appeared to them in their waiting. He arrived in the midst of their longing and encouraged them. He spoke into their doubt. He didn't rebuke their doubt. He told them not to fear, for He would send them comfort and He would come again in victory. He told them to quit pacing, but keep longing.

## the other headphone

Sometimes I think life is in stereo, but we've only been given one headphone. We hear a portion of the song—the high harmony, the kick drum, a hint of tambourine—but nothing leads the way, nothing beckons us to dance.

Some days I think we're subconsciously searching for the other headphone. We sense the disconnect. We miss what's missing. But we're powerless. So, we wait. We listen. We will. We long for the song to come to life.

We wrestle to make sense of conflicting sounds—to force chorus out of chaos—hoping by our effort, the music will become something corporate, something beautiful even.

Other days I wonder if we even realize there's more to the song. I wonder if we've lost our sense of wonder, or if we're too tired to try, or if we're afraid. I wonder if we are afraid to be still—afraid of stillness itself—for if we make time, make stillness, the stillness may speak, the silence may stir, the melody may rise, and we may not like what we hear.

We inhale, but do not breathe deeply. We hear, but do not understand. We see, but it is through stained glass.

We hope of Sunday, but live in Saturday nothing.

Waiting for Jesus is the story of our lives, and it's a story worth telling. In my meantime, there's been melody, mystery, and meaning. There's been trial, hope, and second chances. And there's been Jesus. Always Jesus. He's brought worth to my waiting and my writing.

So welcome to Saturday Nothing, the words I wrote while waiting on Jesus.

# THE CHAPTERS

## 01: the mother

When I was a child, I was afraid of the dark. My mother tells me I had a restless spirit.

Every night I wanted her or my grandmother to tuck me in and say the Lord's Prayer with me. My mom says there were nights when the only way she could get me to stay in bed was reciting the Lord's Prayer over and over until I fell asleep.

I remember those nights. I remember needing to hear something in the room, a fan, a radio, a prayer—anything. I needed to be distracted from the sounds that were out there—the sounds that wanted in—the sounds living in the silence.

My mother was 19, unmarried, Catholic and terrified when she had me. I was born into a world of tradition, tamales, and turmoil. And scented candles. On every shelf and countertop in my grandparents' house was a scented candle with a picture of a saint on it. When someone asked for prayer, you lit a candle to remind yourself to pray, and to make your house smell religious. Sometimes I wonder if one of those scented candles was for me, even before I was born.

My mother tells me abortion never crossed her mind because she had my name picked out for years. The news of her pregnancy was devastating still, but it didn't shake her hope. After the doctor told her she was pregnant, she remembers going home and running to her bedroom, lying face down on her bed and weeping.

She stayed there for what felt like days. She asked God how this could happen, but she got no answer. God felt distant, if even present at all. My mother had already dropped out of high school and now she was pregnant. She told me the weight of it all made her feel like she was drowning.

Eventually, the cloud of judgment lifted, her breath came back, she composed herself, got out of bed and washed her face. As she patted her face dry she looked in a mirror and felt peace wash over her. She placed her hands over her stomach, looked down and said, "Joshua, I guess you're coming sooner than I thought."

My mother tells me she knew I was going to be special, that's why she named me after Joshua in the Bible. Joshua in the Bible became the leader after Moses and led God's people into the Promised Land. My mom says she wanted her son to be that type of person, leading people to that type of place. She would always say, "Joshua, if there's one thing in the world you can trust, it is a promise of God."

My mom worked a lot when I was growing up so my grandparents helped raise me. Sometimes my grandmother would take me to work with her. She was a janitor at a bank. I'd walk in and sit in the big leather chair next to the coffee pots and watch my grandmother vacuum. Every time she turned her back I'd reach up and grab a sugar cube from the box. Then I'd go home and tell my uncle I robbed the bank.

My uncle is only a few years older than me. For years I thought he was my brother. One time he and I were playing one-on-one tackle football in the front yard and he threw me into a tree and an inch of my ear fell off. It probably wasn't an inch, but it bled, so I cried to my grandma. I cried a lot growing up. At least that's what my uncle tells me. I was injured a lot growing up. At least that's what I tell my uncle.

When I was a year old, my mother married for the first time. She says she didn't like the guy much, but she married him to get us out of her parents' house. He was nice enough and able to provide momentary deliverance, which is a selling point for all of us, I think. We all long for rescue.

His name was Kenny. He was no great rescue. Once, he gave me a stuffed monkey named Freddie. It was brown, had long arms and hard black eyes. That's all I remember about that relationship—a stuffed monkey named Freddie. Their marriage didn't last long. After less than a year my mom and I were heading to a new apartment in a new city— again looking for rescue.

My mother's name is Becky. She's 4 foot 11 inches tall, and the most giving person I know. She'll tell you she has a book full of issues and I'll tell you generosity isn't one of them.

If I try, I can hear her laugh, picture her long dark hair and smell the cigarette hanging out of her mouth. What God failed to give my mom in stature He made up for in personality.

Growing up, I remember people wanting to be around my mom; her joy was contagious, which made for a fun home life. Our house had a revolving front door, friends and family were always coming and going. Well, just family really, because that's how my mom saw everyone. If you came to Becky's house, you were never just a friend, and you never left hungry.

My mom is also an artist. She taught me to love music. She would never tell you this, but it's true. On long car rides she would turn on music and sing along, knowing every word. She loved Rod Stewart and Bryan Adams. She would sometimes call radio stations and dedicate songs to me. Other times she'd just tell me this song was my song, then sit me down and play the song for me through the tweed speakers of our old stereo.

My mom taught me how to dance. She said no son of hers would grow up without knowing how to lead a woman around the dance floor.

On more than one occasion I'd come home to our furniture pushed out of the way, Tejano music turned up, and my mom saying, "Come on, show me what I've taught you." The day the young Tejano pop-music star Selena died was a terrible day in our house.

I also remember my mom was handy around the house. She could fix anything, create anything, sew anything, iron anything, and problem solve with the best. And she loved puzzles. Many nights I'd leave the house and have to reach down to kiss my mom because she was on the floor putting together a puzzle. I never helped her. My brother and sister would sometimes, but I never did.

Her puzzles took too long. I always felt like they were a waste of time. I was too young to understand that the puzzle wasn't about the puzzle—it was about spending time with my mom. If I could go back to high school and do one thing differently, I would go back and sit on the floor with my mom and help her put together a puzzle.

My mom wore lots of jewelry and every piece had a story. The gold chain on her neck was a gift from her children on Mother's Day of '96. On her fingers were gold rings she bought from her friend Pam at the pawn shop. On her thumb a "True Love Waits" ring she gave me when I was 14. The ring symbolized my promise to God and my future wife that I would not have sex until I got married. I gave the ring back to my mom when I was 16, after I had broken my promise.

It's not easy telling your mom you lost your virginity. It's not easy saying, "I appreciate the ring, but I feel like a fake wearing it." But I felt fake, so I confessed. After the news was out, my mom hugged me. She didn't judge me. She loved me. She prayed for me.

As I walked away she took the ring and put it on her thumb. To this day she still wears it on her thumb. I once asked why she kept a 30-dollar ring that meant nothing to me. She said, "It's a reminder we are all failures in one way or another, but it doesn't mean we've lost our worth and should be thrown away."

My mom taught me how to love, how to be loyal, how to be inappropriately honest, and how to recklessly give grace. She was my hero growing up. She is my hero even still.

## 02: the father and the other guy

The man I call Dad is 6 foot 4 and his name is Kyle. He's worked in the oil fields all his life. He owns lots of red shirts with a pocket in the front and boots with steel in the toe. 5:00 A.M. is no stranger to him—neither is the terrible Texas heat.

He has calloused hands, a sunburned neckline, and the work ethic of an ox. He loves sports, and comedy, and he knows his way around a poker table. He and my mom married when I was three. They stayed married until I was 17.

Kyle Martin raised me as his own son, taught me to work hard, cheer for the right sports teams, and use proper form on free throws. When I was 16, he adopted me and gave me his last name.

I didn't realize he wasn't my biological father until I was eight. That's when my parents sat me down and told me the story. It was no surprise considering my younger brother and sister were much taller than me, and their complexion much lighter. And I had seen my birth certificate—it was blank where the father's name was supposed to be. One time I almost wrote "God" in the space.

As they broke the news, I didn't feel anything; to me, nothing changed. I now had information that out there somewhere was this other guy who should have his name on my birth certificate, but I didn't care much about him. Whoever he was, wherever he was, didn't interest me.

I played little league football when I was ten and after a game, my mom and I stopped at a gas station in a town near where she grew up. On our way out the door we ran into my biological father. It was like a scene out of a movie. I was holding the door open, he was walking in, and my mom was walking out. Their eyes met in the doorway, separated only by the son they'd made.

I think I was too young to understand the gravity of the situation. I can't imagine what my mother felt when she saw him. I've never asked her. She's never told me. I think I never brought it up because I didn't want her to have to talk about it. The look said enough. I've never seen such shock and pain in her eyes before, and I've never seen it since.

After what felt like eternity, my mom told me to go sit in the car. From inside a blue Ford Astrovan I sat and watched as my mom talked to my dad—a man who was a complete stranger to me. Eventually they walked to the van, slung open the side door, and I was given the grand introduction.

He said hello. I said hello. We shook hands. He smiled. I didn't. It was like meeting an adult my mom worked with—cordial enough, important to her; to me, irrelevance defined.

Looking back, I think my problem was I didn't feel a need for him. Or maybe I wanted to ignore him because he ignored me. I'm still trying to figure it out. My mom tells me when she got pregnant my grandfather threatened to kill him if he came around their house and that's why he stayed away. That didn't matter to me. I had seen enough to know that's not true. If he wanted to see me he could have.

So, there I was, ten years old, in a Stop & Go parking lot in East Texas, still wearing padded football pants and a jersey, sitting in an Astrovan, drinking Sunkist, meeting my long lost father for the first time.

He said he pictured me coming to his door when I was 18, punching him in the nose, and yelling horrible things I had been holding in. He thought that was how we were going to meet. Instead it happened randomly at a gas station, probably a lot like my conception.

As we drove home my mom told me more of the story. I sat there, tapping my football pants with a pencil, looking out the window, daydreaming. I remember Rod Stewart was on the radio singing about the rhythm of his heart and how it was beating like a drum, and his voice mattered to me more than my mother's did.

In the way I saw the world, I already had a father. And he coached me in sports. And he played sports. And he listened to Steve Miller and The Eagles. And he taught me life lessons through his choices. We lived in a racist part of East Texas but my dad never got caught up in that stuff. He didn't see race like others did. He saw things rightly. So, we had a diverse group of friends, and I really liked that. And I really liked the Steve Miller Band.

My current dad made life interesting and fun and competitive and full of laughter and values and perspective. My current dad was the reason I didn't have an emotional reaction to the dad at the gas station. Dad at the gas station was a shadow of the past, a skeleton from a locked closet, a man I didn't know wasting my afternoon with a half-hearted apology.

When I was 16 my biological dad came back into my life by inviting me to his house so he could give me an old truck. The deal was simple. If I helped him fix it, I could have it. I went for a weekend, cleaned some tools, listened to the Goo Goo Dolls on the radio, met some pseudo family members and came home with an old Toyota truck. After about six months the truck broke down and we sold it for parts.

When I was 18, my biological dad showed up to my high school graduation with a video camera. My mother's side of the family also attended graduation, which made for quite the pre-ceremony. My uncle had a couple of beers before commencement and when he saw my biological dad he wanted to go out on the front lawn of the high school, take his shirt off, and defend his sister's honor.

The way it all ended was a simple conversation. My dad told my biological dad filming was fine, but he wanted him to be sure not to go home and tell everyone the kid in the video was his son. He told him not to try and take credit for anything I had accomplished or worked for. He told him he had a chance with me and he didn't take it and that was his loss. My dad needed my biological dad to understand I was not his son. He said, "Josh is my son, and Becky's son, and everything he's achieved, and all he is going to achieve, has nothing to do with you."

My high school graduation was the last time I saw my biological dad.

Even though I wasn't there when the conversation happened, I remember being really proud of my dad for that scene and those words. I remember feeling loved and important.

I remember thinking it would have made for a memorable graduation to see my drunken uncle fight with his shirt off, and his gesture meant a lot to me—because fighting is his love language. I left my graduation realizing my dad and uncle and family loved me. And that's a good feeling at any age.

## 03: the not so great divorce

When I was 17, just eight months prior to graduation, I came out to the parking lot of my high school after football practice and my dad was sitting on the tailgate of his truck next to my little brother. My brother was crying. My parents were splitting up. This was the prologue to a great exodus.

My dad and I switched keys. He told me he was moving a half hour away so he needed my vehicle because it was more reliable. He promised to stay active. He promised to be present. He promised to be there if we needed anything. He promised lots of things.

I don't remember much of what he said, but I remember the lines in his face. He looked tired, deeply wounded, like his soul hurt. I'd never seen my dad like this before. He had been strong, but not anymore. Something changed. Something broke him. He said he and my mom didn't trust each other and he needed to be away for a while.

My parents stayed active in our lives but things shifted. My mom was miserable, depressed, and desperate. She was on her way to the darkest season of her life. My dad was hollow and hurt—his eyes empty. He was working hard to find his identity in doing the right things—stuff like sitting in the bleachers at every sporting event I participated in and coming up afterward and being sure to hug me, look me right in the eyes, and tell me he was proud of me. I don't remember that phrase a whole lot growing up but I remember it became popular around the time he and my mom split.

No matter how hard they tried to make things seem normal, it wasn't normal; life was different. On parents' night for my senior year in football they didn't arrive on time. I had to walk down the track with one of my coaches when my name was called. It was the first moment I realized things were different, and my life was changing in a big way. My parents no longer lived in the same house, they were no longer in love, no longer coming to games together—no longer walking beside me on parents' night.

Divorces are the worst. They crack a foundation. They subtly whisper to kids, "Nothing is secure. Nothing is sacred. Nothing will remain." The trust issues I took into pre-marital counseling were rooted in the trust issues I inherited from my parents. I learned that sitting in a comfy chair across from my wife crying my eyes out. My counselor took my hand and whispered, "You don't have to be like them. You can make it. You can trust."

It's not easy to shake the effects of a broken foundation. It makes your legs wobbly and your head foggy. It makes you question everyone's motives. It makes you harsh and apathetic, jaded and full of angst. It makes you long for stability in someone or something. I remember having a hard time focusing in class; I remember my eyes had a tendency to shift. I remember being tired all the time.

Something about a divorce makes you feel unaccepted. Even though it's not true, it's felt. Our parents left each other and we weren't enough to keep them together. That's what we felt. Thankfully, kids are resilient, faithful beyond reason; otherwise, my parents would have had a hard time holding it together.

## 04: the shame

My beautiful mother faded fast in the wake of the divorce. We were evicted from the four-bedroom house we lived in and forced to move to a trailer across town. I was off to East Texas Baptist University and my brother and sister were both in high school. One of the most surreal things to me was driving home from college, past the house I grew up in, to a trailer less than two miles away—where my family now lived.

My mom fell into a deep depression, and in a timetable still a mystery to me, became addicted to crystal methamphetamine. Over a period of three years she deteriorated right before our eyes. She slept all the time, was gone all the time, and was frustrated all the time. My brother and sister were on their own.

I wish I knew more about what happened with my mom, but I don't. I think that's part of why my heart aches when I think about it. As the oldest, I felt some sort of personal failure. My mom and I always had an honest relationship, always shared with each other the best and the worst of trouble. I felt betrayed when she didn't talk to me, and I felt responsible.

Jennica, my sister, is five years younger than me. She's tough and beautiful and loyal, not easily shaken or shocked. She has my mom's laugh, a heart of hospitality, and my dad's work ethic.

Jeffrey, my brother, is four years younger than me. He's a natural leader with my dad's sense of humor and my mom's welcoming presence. He's strong willed and disciplined and has a faith that is much more than words.

It's hard not to like my brother and sister. They are steady and outgoing and the type of people you want to be friends with. God has given both of them grace and wisdom beyond their years.

Jennica and Jeffrey were forced to grow up quickly though, and there were days when they had to fend for themselves. The humility necessary to ask for rides and money because your parents are elsewhere can wear on a young person. And keeping your eyes up when the shame starts to set in is no easy task. But their faithfulness to my mom never wavered. They led me in moments when I should have led them.

Eventually, my dad moved back to town to help with Jennica and Jeff. It wasn't long before my mom couldn't pay the rent for the trailer. So my dad moved the family to his new place—located a mere block from the home we grew up in. My mom slept on the couch for two years. It was nice for me to come home and see everyone together, but there was still an obvious sense of distrust and lack of love in the home. It was like we were all playing house and keeping quiet about the elephant in the room. It was convenient, I guess.

---

The summer after my college graduation, I got a call from my sister. She was crying and sounded scared. I thought someone died. In a way, someone had. Through tears I heard her say cops had come to my dad's house and found drugs and our mom was in jail.

At the time I was in Colorado leading worship at a summer camp. My brother was in Japan on a mission trip. My sister and dad were the only ones home.

For the first few hours after the call it didn't feel real. I walked around the camp trying to pray and trying to think but mostly feeling helpless. I went to my room and turned on the television. I took a long shower. I dried off slowly. I shaved. I brushed my teeth forever. I put on lotion. I never put on lotion. I was distracting myself or at least trying to.

It wasn't working.

Eventually, I went to the cafeteria with a Bible and a journal, poured myself a cup of coffee, sat still for two minutes, and that's when the pain set in. Like a spirit invading me, the pain came through my back and filled my chest. I felt heavy and empty at the same time. I thought about my mom in jail and I could barely breathe. I opened my journal and wrote to Jesus, and I asked Him to help her. I asked Him to rescue. I asked Him to forgive and redeem and make new. I asked Him to do and be everything I was incapable of doing and being.

My mom spent 48 days in jail. When my summer job was over the family pooled together the money we had and were able to bail her out. For some reason, I remember being angry with God. I remember feeling a lot of shame. Prayers of rescue quickly turned to fear and a need to save face. I wasn't in Colorado anymore. I was home. And at home I had an image to maintain.

From fourth grade until graduation I grew up in a city of 1,000 people. News like this was humiliating, and a popular topic of conversation. Truth is, I was afraid of losing the reputation I thought I had. I went away to a Christian College. I had just finished my degree in Biblical Studies. I was going into ministry. I shouldn't have a mom in jail. This wouldn't look good on my résumé. I was foolish, insecure, afraid, and acting nothing like Jesus. This was a shameful time in my story, and a season in which God really disciplined me.

I remember having a conversation with God about all of it. First, we talked about money. I remember telling Him I worked hard that summer and earned that money and I needed that money and it was rightfully mine.

God doesn't speak to me audibly. He impresses things on my heart, reveals things in my head and sometimes, if I'm so fortunate, burns things into my soul. This was a soul moment.

The Lord reminded me of the story of the woman caught in adultery—how she was thrown naked at the feet of Jesus and how Jesus was not ashamed of her. The Lord reminded me of how Jesus knelt down to her level, took her side, stood up to the teachers of the law on her behalf, and then—without condemnation—inspired her to go and leave her life of sin. And everything in me believed the woman in that story never went back to her old ways. Everything in me believes when you look into the eyes of Jesus and you're given an invitation to a better story, you take it. You can't resist.

Then the Lord was extremely stern with me. He filled my heart with this truth: I had chosen to disassociate myself with my mother rather than run to her rescue. Turns out, I'm a horrible rescue as well. This was too much to bear. The fact was, in my mother's deepest time of need, I chose myself over her. I took the avenue of abandonment and self-preservation, rather than love and reckless loyalty.

Now I was ashamed of myself, not my mom.

About the money, God was very gentle. In the midst of my tears He revealed simply, almost in a whisper, "Josh, about this money you earned, since when is anything yours? Everything is mine. Everything you have is mine."

I remember feeling a real brokenness and nearness to Jesus. I remember He was terribly tangible. I remember telling God I was sorry and telling my mom I was sorry and looking her in the face and telling her I wasn't ashamed of her. I had no condemnation for her. I remember in the exchange with my mother, the Spirit of the Lord spoke those same words to my heart—He was not ashamed of me, and neither did He condemn me.

## 05: the eyes of Jesus

When I was 15, my mom and I were baptized together. She had given up her Catholic roots and began attending another church and it wasn't long before Jesus captivated her heart. Being      baptized with my mom is one of the most beautiful memories of my life.

Prior to getting arrested, my mom worked for seven years as a translator and bookkeeper in the jail she served time in. The irony was sickening to her. She told me people always found God in jail. She said Jesus really liked jail church because people were actually honest, actually guilty, and those were the kind of people who could be changed.

While she was serving her time and even throughout her drug addiction and depression my mom said Jesus was always with her. She said some nights she would have dreams of Him calling her home. She said many nights she'd wake up in a cold sweat and feel His presence. She said Jesus saved her life on more than one occasion.

My mom went to jail church while she was in jail. She said at jail church they have a lot of confession time where people talk about their struggles, their sin, their tendencies, and afterward, they pray for each other. She said they pray a lot in jail church. My mom told me one day she found the courage to speak up and she shared with the people in jail church about Jesus always being there—how He showed up in her dreams and when she was cold in her cell she would feel His presence.

While she was speaking, she said other inmates shook their heads and said, "Me too." Evidently, Jesus was near to these women. They all had similar stories and each of them was even willing to say they were grateful God allowed them to get caught.

It all reminded me of a story in the Old Testament. The one where Abraham and Sarah go into a city and in fear of death, they lie and say Sarah is not Abraham's wife but rather his sister. The king then takes Sarah into his chambers and that night has a terrifying dream.

In the dream God comes to the king and tells him He is going to destroy him and his entire kingdom. The king is afraid and asks God why this is going to happen. God tells him it's because he is sleeping with another man's wife. The king says, "I didn't know," and God responds with something overwhelming. God says, "I know, that is why I tell you now, for I am not going to let you sin against me anymore."

My mom is a testimony of the unstoppable nature and power of God. There was a time when He looked into my mother's life and said, "Alright, enough. I'm not going to let you sin against me anymore."

---

In college, I had a Biblical Interpretation professor named Dr. Bob. Dr. Bob always talked about being skeptical of people who said Jesus showed up to them in a certain place and time. He said when he was a pastor, people would call him and say Jesus showed up in the hospital room with them when they were thinking about giving up.

He went on to say he'd been in the hospital before, and Jesus didn't appear to him. Therefore, Jesus must not have come to those people. He would ask if they were having indigestion or on strong medication.

Then Dr. Bob said he started thinking about it. He started thinking about the character of God and the life of Jesus. Dr. Bob said if there was a person hurting in the hospital, feeling hopeless, wanting to give up, that this sounded like the type of scenario Jesus would love to show up in. It seemed just because this hadn't happened to him had nothing to do with whether or not it was possible.

I remembered Dr. Bob's story when my mom told me about Jesus in jail. I remember picturing my mom lying there in a barren room tortured by detox, with little comfort, no privacy, ashamed, cold, and miserable. I remember picturing Jesus the Great Physician being there, healing her, comforting her, sitting on the side of her bed, praying over her, running His hand through her hair and across the sheets she laid under, whispering truth to her, breathing life into her lifeless state. I remember thinking this situation seemed like the perfect fit for Jesus.

I remembered in the Bible a place where Jesus spoke about giving water and clothing to those in need and in doing so, you were somehow doing it unto Him. I remembered He talked about visiting people in jail in the same text. I remembered thinking that it seemed so out of place. Then I looked at my mom through a window—talked to her using a telephone though we were hardly a foot apart. In that moment I realized what Jesus meant.

He was already there, already doing the hard work of reconciliation. But, Jesus wants us to come and to see Him there, to join Him in what He is already doing.

Looking at my mom there, in that place, through that window, on that phone, for those few minutes, may have been the first time I did something for Jesus. It certainly was the first time I looked into His eyes.

## 06: the heart of God

Sometimes when it's overcast outside, or cold and rainy, I think about what my life would be if Jesus had not sat beside my bed, sang truth over me, and on more than one occasion saved my life. I think I would be a father who did not know his kids, a guy who mistreated women, an extremely insecure and frustrated man who didn't appreciate a good cup of coffee, music, or art. I think without Jesus continually being my rescue I would have become everything I currently hate. There are times when even now, before my eyes, I see traces of becoming what I hate. I think the season with my mom was an aggressive look in the mirror—a time when Jesus reminded me of who He wanted me to be and how far I was from it.

---

In the Old Testament there was a king named David. He's the lead role in the greatest underdog story of all time. He killed Goliath. I've always wondered what it would feel like to cut the head off a giant. The Bible also says David was a man after God's own heart. I've always wondered what it meant to be a man after God's own heart and what kind of heart an invisible God has.

One summer King David decides not to go off to war with his

men like he's supposed to. Instead he takes some time off, and sits on the couch for a while. During his vacation, King David commits adultery with a woman named Bathsheba.

She gets pregnant and David gets nervous. He calls Bathsheba's husband, Uriah, in from war and tries to get him drunk, in hopes that he will have sex with his wife and the pregnancy can be concealed. But the plan doesn't work. Uriah refuses to sleep with Bathsheba while his men are off at war. Even in his drunkenness he is noble enough to sleep on the front porch. So, in response, David orders Uriah to the front line of battle, sentencing him to death.

David is the leader of Israel—an alleged man after God's own heart. Yet he's a liar, an adulterer, and a murderer.

David has a friend named Nathan the Prophet. God appointed certain men, called prophets, to speak for Him and Nathan was one of these men. He had divine insight and authority and the ability to speak hard truth. It was Nathan the Prophet's job to hear a word from God and give the word to the people. And sometimes God gave brilliant ways to deliver the news.

So, Nathan the Prophet goes to David one afternoon and tells him a story of two men. One man is rich and has limitless sheep at his disposal. The other man is poor and has only one lamb in his possession. The man with one lamb loves his lamb so much he sleeps with it, cares for it, and would give up his life for it. Nathan the Prophet says a guest comes to the rich man's house and, instead of preparing one of his many sheep, the rich man goes to the poor man and steals his only lamb, kills it, and uses it to prepare dinner for his guest.

David becomes enraged by the story and demands that Nathan the Prophet bring the rich man to him for he must face judgment and death four times over for his actions. Then, as any good epic goes, the music fades, the camera zooms in, everything goes into slow motion, and Nathan the Prophet draws near to David, puts a finger in his chest, and tells the King of Israel, "You are that man."

---

     I think David is a man after God's own heart because he understood something many of us don't. David understood confession. He understood that when you're confronted with truth you shouldn't run the other way or deflect or defend. You should bear the responsibility of your sin. You should walk with a limp for the rest of your life before you walk with lies.

     When David has Nathan's finger in his chest he breaks. He says, "You're right, I've sinned against God." David understood God. He trusted God. He knew if he confessed his brokenness, he'd find God's forgiveness. David knew God's grace in an inspired way. After the sin and after the confrontation, something deep inside of David told him not to hide from God, but rather make God his hiding place. This concept is truly foreign to me. I'm a runner—a runner slowly learning to run towards God, not away, learning to make Him my hiding place, not who I hide from.

## 07: the question

Faith has always been a part of who I am. Over the years it's been a bed of peace, and a bed of nails, but it's always where I lay my head.

The church I attended growing up was small and simple, filled with pews, Sunday school rooms, and the smell of faithfulness. We sang hymns every Sunday—Norman's wife Laurie could play every hymn in the book. Those people taught me how to follow Jesus. My love for God, my knowledge of the Bible, and my understanding of prayer have all been built on a foundation laid in that church.

Every summer our youth group went to a leadership camp in East Texas. Most times it was the greatest week of my year. I'd hold in all my issues and tears and frustrations and let them out at camp, over those five days. One summer though, when I was 16, I was at camp and it was Thursday and I hadn't cried yet. As trivial as it may seem, this, for me, was a crisis. God was emotion, and I was cold as stone. I couldn't feel Him like the others, I couldn't cry like the others; so, the nothing I felt led me to believe God must not be real.

I became a non-believer right there at summer camp. I told my group leader I needed to talk to him because I wanted out, and someone needed to give me a ride home. I knew the truth, or had recently learned the truth—God's not real—which meant everyone at camp was crazy for crying and worshipping and confessing. No more would I be counted among the crazies.

I told my leader I had a new confession and I wouldn't let the blanket be pulled over my eyes any longer. I was smarter than this whole thing and he should be too. It was all made up. I had figured it out. And I said, "On another note, group leader, I don't think Jesus was real, either. Not that I don't think he was the Son of God or the resurrection happened—I don't believe he existed. He and God both live in a world of non-existence."

I was a melodramatic teenager. Either the world was caving in on my head or it was the most beautiful gift I had ever received. I was having a bad day. I had very little gray area to live in. Things were simple then.

My group leader listened to my speech and didn't say much. He shook his head in a way of saying he was listening, not in a way of saying he agreed with me. He stayed compassionate up to the "Jesus wasn't real" part.

When I said Jesus didn't exist my group leader took his Bible, walked across the room and set it on a table. As he walked back he told me it was one thing to have issues with the existence of God and the divinity of Jesus, and the trustworthiness of the Bible, but to say Jesus didn't exist was ridiculous and historically ignorant.

Even though he said it lovingly, I had never been called ignorant before. It didn't feel good. He told me even outside of the Bible there are writings about a man named Jesus. He told me Jesus really lived for 33 years or so and he was killed on a Roman cross. He said saying Jesus wasn't a real person was like saying WWI was not a real war or George Washington was not a real president. He told me to go to the library.

Eventually he softened up a bit and said, "Josh, I'm grateful you are thinking about this stuff, but in the end you are still going to have to answer one question: What are you going to do with Jesus?"

After a few hours I took back my faith. But I remember it felt different—better—more tangible. After my short stint in the hotel of non-belief I found Jesus more accessible. I found His job as a carpenter more inspiring, His death more agonizing. When my counselor told me Jesus really lived—and the library could attest—it made everything in the Bible so much more relevant. The Bible was no longer a bunch of random stories or a road map to live by or some instruction manual. It was alive. It had breath. This basic revelation turned every word of the Bible into an arrow pointing to Jesus. And if Jesus was real, He was capable of changing everything.

It may seem elementary to have had my affection stirred simply by being told Jesus existed, but it happened. My doubts melted under the news of a historical Jesus. I had no problem with the divine nature, virgin birth or sinless life of Jesus—once I realized He actually lived and died in a specific time in human history. I remember re-visiting my Bible and being overwhelmed by the words in red. I remember they looked different. Somehow, they spoke more clearly. They were now the words of God, spoken in human history by the only man who was God. It was more than I could handle.

I went into the worship service that night at camp and was hardly able to mouth the lyrics of the songs. I was so enthralled by the news. I wanted to tell the guy next to me Jesus was real. I wanted to ask him if he had ever really thought about it. He probably had, so I left him alone.

The music played my heart back to life. Each word drew me into a relationship. A relationship I never really knew I had. I always thought I had an ideal, a set of beliefs, or eternal assurance, but that night I knew I had a person. That night when I was finally able to sing, I sang my heart out to a person.

During the sermon, the preacher talked about Jesus meeting a Samaritan woman at a well during the hottest part of the day. I remember for the first time I didn't think of it as some story in some fairy tale someone made up. I found it to be human and true and gritty and beautiful. Jesus was God in the flesh. He got tired and thirsty. He asked a prostitute for a drink of water. He had friends who went and got Him lunch. This moved me in my soul. It made me wonder, made me sit in awe. It propelled me to worship, and made me want to give my life for His mission. This Jesus was real. And I believed I could trust Him.

## 08: the unbelief

Even now the red letters overwhelm me. The stories Jesus told, the inter-actions He had, the people He healed and changed are so real and power-ful.

My favorite story of Jesus is a short interaction recorded in Mark chapter 9. A man runs to Jesus and says an evil spirit has possessed his son. The evil spirit is trying to kill him and is causing great anguish. The father asks Jesus if He can do anything to help. Jesus responds, "If I can? Anything is possible for those who believe." Almost before Jesus is fin-ished speaking, the man cries out, "I believe, Lord; help my unbelief." Jesus immediately calls for the man's son to be brought forward and He heals him. Jesus never belittles the man for his confession of unbelief. Jesus takes the confession of belief with the confession of unbelief to be enough. Jesus shows the father and his son great mercy and compassion because of honesty, not faith.

It reminds me of Matthew chapter 28 when Jesus gives The Great Commission.

"Now the eleven disciples went to Galilee, to the mountain to which Jesus had directed them. And when they saw Him they worshiped Him, but some doubted. And Jesus came and said to them, "All authority in heaven and on earth has been given to me. Go therefore and make disciples of all nations, baptizing them in the name of the Father and of the Son and of the Holy Spirit, teaching them to observe all that I have commanded you. And behold, I am with you always, to the end of the age."

Of the 120 people on the mountain to hear and receive His words, some doubted, yet Jesus gave the commission anyway. It was almost as if He was saying, "I understand right now you are doubting, but you will soon come around. I'll help your unbelief. In the meantime, I need you to understand something. In the midst of your doubts I still need you to clearly hear my mission. I need you to hear what I want my church to be."

Jesus healed the man's demonic son and in so doing, helped his unbelief more than a thousand sermons could. He gave the commission and in so doing called unbelievers to believe.

Even today, in the echo of an ever-ringing great commission, I would love to have the strength to look at God and say, "I'm struggling, will You help me, I am a skeptic at heart. I can't help it. I want to believe, but I have so much unbelief. Today, I need to touch and see the scars like Thomas did, would You allow grace for that?"

Jesus said it's the wicked generations who need to see signs and wonders to believe. The book of Hebrews defines faith as trusting in the unseen. But even still Jesus is gentle toward the doubter, patient with those willing to admit their fears, kind to those who ask to see. The skeptic always had a seat at Jesus' table.

Those stories of doubt have always been the ones that feel like the middle cushion of our living room couch to me. I'm comfortable with doubt stories. I've sat in them before—many times. I know how to put my feet up and stay a while. The same with struggle, it's like the old shirt I go to in my closet even though I've been given ten new ones.

I think most days we could change the world if we woke up and admitted, "Jesus I believe; help my unbelief."

---

In the prequel to the 1970's horror film The Exorcist, the protagonist is a man who was a priest but renounced his faith and became an archeologist. He ends up in the middle of Africa—in the place where Satan allegedly landed when he was cast out of heaven. He's studying rocks and old churches when crazy stuff starts to happen.

In the climax of the movie, the possessed person kills the only priest in the area and runs into an underground tunnel. The ex-priest turned archeologist goes to the now dead priest and begins to weep. Then the weeping turns to anger, then to remembrance, then to action. The archeologist takes the sash from the dead priest, borrows his Bible and his cross necklace and puts it all on himself.

Then he does something I will never forget. He puts his head down for a minute, the music changes, he runs his fingers across the sash, he kisses the cross, grips tightly the Bible, looks up with tears in his eyes, and with brokenness in his voice says, "Lord I believe; help my unbelief." Then he ducks his head and disappears into the cave.

Even now I remember that scene like it was played for me this morning—mostly because it was. It plays for me every morning. Most days I think I would make a better archeologist than a priest. Most days I doubt my calling, my ability—my everything. Most days I think it would help if I put my head down, cried a little, kissed a cross, gripped the Bible, asked for help, and headed into the darkness.

## 09: the awakening

The majority of my understanding of Jesus came from people who were willing to live out faith in front of me. I read people, and in so doing, in some way, read the Bible.

During my junior high and high school years, I split time between two churches. One was a small Baptist church and the other was a larger non-denominational charismatic congregation. Prior to this, I was frequenting a Catholic church in a town 15 miles away from where I lived. My mom and grandma took me to Catholic church when I was young. But what do you really remember before you're ten? So, when we moved to our new city I would go to Catholic church on occasion, to honor Grandma.

As an 11-year-old, I made it through confession and first communion in the Catholic confirmation process. When the wine touched my lips it was my first taste of strong alcohol. When the priest told me to do my first bunch of prayers for cheating on a spelling test and beating up my little brother, it was my first taste of wanting out of the system.

I remember going home and doing my prayers all at once in my bedroom and still feeling terrible about that test and my brother. If God needed me to pray over and over the same words to be granted forgiveness then it seemed I would have a long life of repetition. I was not okay with that. I came out of my bedroom and told my mom I didn't want to go back to confession. I wanted to confess my sins directly to God. I told her I was sorry she had just bought me a new Rosary but I didn't want it anymore. She hugged me, told me she loved me and the Rosary was cheap, and I never had to go back to church.

After that hug from my mother I spent a year at a church but not in a church. What I mean is, the Baptist church a few blocks from my house was the only place with a decent basketball court. So, every Sunday afternoon, very religiously, at 12:30 all the people dressed nicely would come out of the building, get into their cars and drive to a local restaurant. Then all the kids on bikes with their shirts off drinking Sunkist would come and play basketball.

One week a man named Norman—Laurie the piano player's husband—was there at the basketball courts. He told me about a Wednesday night youth group at another church. He said if I wanted to go he would give me a ride, because he drove the van. Norman was married to the mom of my best friend and on-again/off-again junior high girlfriend Emily, so I trusted him and was interested in the ride. For the next few months, I rode to church every Wednesday and Sunday in a big grey van. When summer came Norman told me he had paid my way to a summer camp if I wanted to go.

My mother has always been loyal to me. She led me and let me lead. She was perfectly balanced in this, always knowing where to draw the line. When I told her I wanted to go to camp, she was happy to see me happy. Her Catholic roots were fading but her trust in God wasn't. She sent me to camp with joy, and more candy than any other kid.

At the time all I knew about the Baptist church Norman brought me to was they liked food, ping-pong, meetings, and talking about lists of people who needed prayer. All I knew about myself was I liked girls, ping-pong, nachos, basketball, and sleeping places that were not my parents' house. This camp offered just about everything I was into. Except for the ladies. Turns out it was an R.A. camp, which stands for Royal Ambassadors, which stands for a camp with no ladies.

On the upside, I became a certified canoe guide and learned how to shoot a .22 rifle. I also learned Norman served as a sniper in the U.S. Army. During our shooting sessions, everyone in our cabin would take turns shooting and making fun of Norman's mullet.

Then one day Norman shot with us. We all took five shots, then went and got our target. Norman's target came back with one hole right in the middle. I asked if he missed four times and hit it once. He looked at me and said, no, he hit it all five times. I said I didn't understand. He said, "I use to be a... Never mind, you wouldn't understand." Later someone told me he was a sniper in the Army. I never made fun of his mullet again.

Every night at R.A. camp we would go into this big building called The Tabernacle and sing songs and listen to someone talk about Jesus. Then we would be let out for late-night nachos and ping-pong. I was 12 years old. I was not necessarily a rebellious kid but I was also not the kid who was very interested in what was happening. I sat against the back wall most services and served more as a spectator than a participator.

All I knew about God up to this point, due to my previous Catholic experience, was we were to be quiet around Him. God didn't like kids talking. And when you were in God's house you were to kneel and do a sign of the cross over your heart before you sat in your chair. The God I knew was into rituals. Most of the time I couldn't keep up with all He wanted. The first time I came into The Tabernacle at R.A. camp I walked around looking for the holy water. They didn't have any.

This church camp God was different. The songs had hand motions, the preachers tried to be funny, and at the end of every talk there was a portion where we were to bow our head and close our eyes. If we wanted to accept Jesus—whatever that meant—we were to raise our hand while no one was looking.

Tabernacle time wasn't so bad. I just didn't find it important. I was interested in other things. I was still learning about this new God. I liked basketball and shooting guns and looking at my canoe license and working on my flying squirrel off the diving board. The lifeguard was the only girl on campus, which was probably why I wanted so badly to master the dive.

The awakening happened for me when an elderly couple came in one afternoon for a special assembly. They had been missionaries for 40 years in Brazil. All of us smelly boys gathered in The Tabernacle on a hot Thursday afternoon in Texas and we listened to these people talk.

For whatever reason my heart was different that hour. I wasn't thinking about the lifeguard or about Norman being able to kill me from a mile away or about how great it felt to have a canoe license. I was sitting there and it felt like time was standing still. My heart and mind were attentive.

There was no singing for this session, no hand motions, no jokes, no heads bowed, no eyes closed, no hands raised. The only thing on the stage was a bright smiling couple in their 60's standing next to a table full of memories from Brazil. I remember there being a huge snakeskin on the table and how I couldn't wait until they got to that part of the story.

For an hour these two beautiful people told of their life and how, when they were just a little older than our age, they felt a call from God to go and speak of His love in other countries. They talked about meeting each other, falling in love, getting an education together, getting married, and they spoke of the evening in which they got on their knees and asked God if Brazil was where they should go.

I was captivated by their love for each other and their love for this God. During the part of their presentation when they talked about praying on their knees asking God to direct them they reached out and held hands.

These people had it figured out. They were telling me the greatest story I had ever heard. Between each memory they looked at each other and smiled and remembered and breathed deeply. Toward the end of their presentation I could not even remember why the snakeskin mattered. All I wanted to know was when I could go to Brazil and when I could have an adventure like that in my own life. I was already looking around for the sign-up sheet.

They finished their presentation by telling us about the worth of Jesus, and how all they had done was for the name of Jesus and for the glory of God. They said they had given their life to this cause and now wanted to share their testimony and encourage others to do the same. They wanted to challenge others to forsake everything for this Jesus. Even at 60 and after a life of service they were still obsessed with Jesus.

For the rest of the afternoon I couldn't get over those missionaries. I had never thought of God as this wonderful before. Never had I seen or heard of people giving up their entire lives to spread the word of God in other countries. Honestly, I never knew God was worth so much.

That night in The Tabernacle I raised my hand, walked forward, and asked a counselor if he could tell me the story of Jesus and why He was worth so much. For the next hour I sat on a ping-pong table and listened to the Gospel. I had heard it before, but not like this. Either my heart was ready or this counselor was incredibly clear. Either way, it didn't feel as rule heavy. This was relational. As he told me again the story of Jesus, my heart came to life.

I remember feeling energy; like, if right then we lined up all the kids at camp and had a race, I would outrun everyone. I felt light and inspired and overwhelmed and emotional and special. The counselor and I prayed and things internally changed for me. I remember hugging Norman after talking to the counselor. I told him I decided to follow Jesus. Norman, through tears, told me he was proud of me.

That week at R.A. camp in Newton, Texas, some missionaries in their 60's told me a story bigger than anything I had ever heard. They told me of a carpenter from Nazareth who—in the best possible way—ruined their life. Now He had ruined mine, and continues to do so even to this day.

## 10: the great exchange

Martin Luther called the cross of Christ "The Great Exchange"—the place where Jesus and humanity switched place, status, and standing. The implication is on a transaction—a dual nature, a substitution—a final scene in the grandest of courtrooms.

Recently I watched a video of a guy named R.C. Sproul teaching on a doctrine called imputed righteousness. In the video, R.C. Sproul is wearing a blue tie and a sports coat. The people in the crowd have big hair, tinted glasses, and most of the men have a mustache. The video was made in the early 1980's.

During the teaching, R.C. Sproul walks over and draws two circles on a chalkboard. One circle he fills in. The other he leaves empty. The colored circle represents the sin of humanity. The empty circle represents the perfection of Jesus.

R.C. Sproul says in the cross, all of humanity's sin-filled circle was given over to Jesus. He says the circle full of sin is imputed to Jesus on the cross. Then R.C. Sproul takes his chalk and colors in the circle representing Jesus and leaves both circles full. Then R.C. Sproul puts down the chalk and walks away from the board.

He paces the room for a minute looking at the floor. After a few laps he looks up, grabs his podium and with audacity says, "Being forgiven is not the point of the cross." He starts to raise his voice and says the great exchange is not so much about the sin of humanity being put on Jesus but rather the miracle of the Gospel is—he runs back to the chalkboard and with urgency erases the filling of circle number one—in turn Jesus gives over—imputes—all of his righteousness onto those who believe.

R.C. Sproul says in the cross, Jesus is both the wrath-bearing Substitute and the grace-giving Savior. Jesus fully took on our sin and fully gave away His righteousness and in so doing, God the Father is fully satisfied in His love and justice.

R.C. Sproul says forgiveness will only keep you out of hell, not get you into heaven. He says the only thing that gets people into heaven is righteousness. R.C. Sproul says being a Christian means you believe God really put all of your sin on Jesus and Jesus really put all of His righteousness on you.

The simple truth of those circles is soul stirring.

Jesus put it like this, "Unless your righteousness is greater than that of the Pharisees, you will never taste the Kingdom of God." Where we sometimes miss it is when we think Jesus is saying act better, be better, try harder. When the truth is, Jesus is saying He alone is righteous. He alone can stand before the Father fully confident. Sinclair Ferguson says it well, "When you understand the only righteousness you have is Jesus, you can stand before God as confident as Jesus."

---

In John chapter 5, Jesus has a haunting interaction with the Pharisees. Typically Jesus is harsh with the religious types, or at least it would seem, but in the Bible you don't get the tone of voice. One can assume pretty clearly the connotations of the conversation, but nonetheless one can only assume.

In John 5 Jesus looks at the Pharisees and teachers of the Law and says, you men know the Torah, the Law, the Old Testament, and the

Prophets better than anyone. You have it memorized; yet, here I stand before you, the Messiah, the fulfillment of the Law and the Prophets, and you refuse to come to me to have life.

He says to them, everything our fathers waited on, everything you're waiting for is here now, in front of you—in me—and you're missing it. In all of your knowledge you have failed to see the Father's greatest revelation. You must die to the belief that the Law saves.

Jesus pleads with the religious. I imagine the Son of God speaking with arms out—entreatment in his voice—giving these brilliant men an opportunity to respond. He needed them to understand their righteousness was insufficient, but their study not in vain. He wanted their learning to collide with faith. Fulfillment was among them and Jesus was inviting them to connect the dots.

He does the same thing in Luke 15.

The chapter starts by saying sinners and tax collectors drew near to hear Jesus. They felt welcome. The socially outcast and religiously ostracized wanted to get close to Jesus—because He was good news. He included them. He was a teacher who didn't treat them like they were invisible.

Jesus told His best three parables that day. He had a good crowd so He gave them good stories. Of the three—the most well-known—is the story of the prodigal son. Rightfully so. For Jesus to tell a group of sinners and tax collectors, "God is willing to run out and meet you and throw you a party and give you a ring even though you have betrayed your birthright and now smell like a pig pen," is glorious and unexpected. It was tried and true Jesus.

Lord knows I have needed that story many times. Even now it moves me to imagine a God who is patient and waits for and rejoices in every prodigal who comes home. It's certainly good news.

But the interesting thing is, at the end of the story, the father leaves the party and goes out and entreats the older brother. He tells him with compassion to come in and celebrate.

I like to think during this part of the story Jesus looked right at the Pharisees and spoke directly to them, "You have always been with me, everything I have has always been yours, please join the party. Come, leave your bitterness, hear the music of redemption, do not be too self-righteous to dance."

## 11: the apostle and the martyr

The next summer—as a 13-year-old—I went back to Royal Ambassadors camp in Newton. I again raised my hand during the head down eyes closed portion of the program. But this time my ping-pong table conversation with the counselor was different. I was already a follower of Jesus, and I had spent a year faithfully riding the bus to church. But the games and food weren't the only things drawing me now.

Over that year I learned following Jesus was bigger than one day a week. I learned you could do more for God than just go to church, and I wanted in on it. What I was feeling now was what the preacher described as a "call to ministry." I told the counselor I don't want a real job. I want to work for Jesus full time. I asked if there were any openings at his church.

Looking back I don't know if I would word things that way again. I guess what I am trying to say is, I think a call into full-time ministry is great, but not a necessary component to fulfilling the Great Commission. Whatever job you have, you can do it for God's glory. The different jobs we have and roles we play, in and out of church, are beautiful and important, but at the baseline of every job or role—for the Christian—is the same story, the same ministry. The ministry of reconciliation is what I'm getting at—at least that is what the apostle Paul called it.

Paul was not always an apostle. He was once Saul, a devout Jew with a résumé capable of embarrassing anyone in comparison. Too bad God is not interested in résumés, or at least not interested in the way we may think.

In college, Dr. Bob told us of a scenario that played out over and over in his head. In the scenario he was standing before God and was being asked the question, "Why should you be allowed into my heaven?" Dr. Bob told us if this ever happened and this question was ever asked of him, he knew exactly what he would and wouldn't say and do. He knew he wouldn't pull out his résumé and hand it to God. Dr. Bob said he wouldn't tell God he had been a pastor for a long time and taught the Bible to college students for an even longer time. He said he would not list any of his achievements.

Dr. Bob said if he were asked the question why he should be allowed into heaven, he would look God in the face and say with all the confidence a human heart can muster, and maybe even a pointed finger, "I get in, because You promised."

I always thought that was a crazy story and that God probably wouldn't like to have a finger pointed at Him and that God might not mind taking a look at Dr. Bob's résumé. In my mind, even our résumé could tell of God's glory.

The more I thought about it though, the more I realized just how much this answer spoke of trust, and just how much God truly wants his children, pastors, and bible college teachers to trust Him.

If Dr. Bob ever had this metaphor play out, and he pointed at God and told Him, "I'm in, because You promised," I think God would rejoice in that, smile even, cross His cosmic arms, lean back in His cosmic chair and say, "Good answer, Bob, that's a really good answer."

I think God loves when people trust His promises.

When Saul comes on the scene, he is about the same age Jesus was when he died. The problem with Saul is he had a problem with the promise. Saul did not believe the promises of God could have been about Jesus of Nazareth. In Saul's thinking, Jesus was nothing more than a false prophet who hijacked the story and led people away from the God of the Covenant.

Saul believed Jesus was dead and got what He deserved. So, in response to this new movement of Christ followers, Saul took his influence and rage, and turned it toward the destruction of those who followed Jesus.

In the book of Acts, Saul gives approval to the stoning of a young man named Stephen who served as a deacon in the early church. Saul was there, heavily involved—a leading influence—in the first time someone gave their life for the name of Jesus.

Something interesting happens right before Stephen's death. Before the rocks start flying, Stephen preaches a sermon about Jesus as Messiah. His words of truth and insults of brilliance drive his persecutors over the edge. And as the execution begins, Stephen boldly says, "Look, I see the Son of Man standing at the right hand of God."

What's so scandalous about those words is they are the only recorded time when anyone references Jesus as, "Standing at the right hand of God." Every other text says He is sitting at the right hand of God.

The difference between descriptions is important because sitting spoke of being finished. Sitting is a reference to the Old Testament ceremony called The Day of Atonement—when once a year the high priest would perform his duties and, upon completion, sit.

In sitting, the priest was telling the community the sin of the people had both been paid for and sent away. The hearts and consciences of the people could feel at ease once the priest sat down. The payment was over. Sin was paid for and exiled. All was right with God.

To speak of Jesus sitting at the right hand of God signified He too was finished. This language is in unison with His final words on the cross being, "It is finished." In Aramaic, even today, this phrase Jesus muttered on the cross is what people use to let the trash man know he can take their trash away. The phrase "it is finished" was commonly spoken of as "paid in full."

If Jesus sits down, then He is eternally saying what I've accomplished is never to be done again, for it was done well this time, done once, done for all, done sufficiently. Jesus sitting is a significant sitting, and therefore Jesus rising to His feet is a significant rising.

Stephen gave a speech about Jesus and was killed and rewarded for it. In his last breath, Stephen looked up and saw the Savior of the world giving him a standing ovation. Before Stephen closed his eyes and fell asleep he witnessed the Kingdom of Heaven become actual. He saw his meantime disappear. Jesus met Stephen in his waiting. And Stephen had eyes to see.

What's interesting is, Stephen doesn't mention Jesus saying anything when he stands. The book of Acts just says He stands. Jesus does not supernaturally stop the rocks. He does not give a speech. He does not tell Stephen anything. Jesus simply stands.

Many years before this day a Psalmist wrote, "Precious in the sight of the Lord is the death of His saints." Seems Jesus was on His feet to witness something precious, something everlasting—the death of a saint for the sake of His Name. As Stephen ushered in the new reality of martyrdom, Saul stood to witness, and so too Jesus stood to witness, not only the martyr, but also the foreshadowing.

Jesus stood to set a precedent. When people lay down their lives for Him, they do so under a standing ovation.

Something about that speech and that afternoon was too much for Saul. He started with Stephen and was now bent on purifying the people of God by ridding them of the people of Jesus. So Saul goes to the high priest and asks for permission to take on a new job. He even draws up his own job description. He is going to travel around—seek out—and kill families who follow the way of Jesus.

The writer of the book of Acts is a doctor named Luke, and Luke says Saul goes from town to town ravaging the church, breathing out murderous threats. Saul was a nightmare to the first century church. Saul thought what he was doing was right. Saul thought he was honoring God.

On his way to the city of Damascus, Saul has an unexpected, aggressive encounter with Jesus. Jesus appears in a beam of light, throws Saul to the ground, strikes him blind, terrifies his companions, and in brilliant Jesus fashion, starts the exchange with a question: "Saul, why do you persecute me?" Saul doesn't understand. He is still on the ground trying to catch his breath, probably bleeding, his eyes on fire, his heart racing. Somehow he finds a way to say, "Who are you? Are you the Lord?"

At this point Saul is asking if this is the voice of God, the voice of the Lord. Jesus responds with, "It is I, Jesus, the Lord, the One whom you are persecuting." Jesus tells Saul, the God you think you are serving is the same God I am. Jesus moves the conversation right along by giving a few instructions to Saul on what is about to happen in his life. In a final word, Jesus says, "Saul, your name will now be Paul, and I am going to show you how much you must suffer for my Name."

Everything in the book of Acts was about this Name.

When Jesus shows up to Saul turned Paul, I get the same feeling I get when God shows up to the king who was about to sleep with Abraham's wife in the Old Testament. Jesus says emphatically, "I'm not going to let you sin against me anymore, Saul." Whether it is food, water, or even persecution, if we give it, we are not just giving to those receiving. We are also, always, somehow giving to Jesus. He is everywhere, in everyone, able to be served or persecuted.

## 12: the road and three days

The trouble with the God of the Bible is He can be extremely intrusive. Sometimes meeting Him is far more like a collision than a calm walk down the aisle in a tabernacle in East Texas. Sometimes it's a train wreck of worldviews. Sometimes we walk away limping, bleeding, our eyes on fire, and going by a new name. Sometimes we are given sight, sometimes we are blinded; both in hopes that we may see. Sometimes we barely feel alive. Sometimes we have never felt more alive.

This is what happens in conversion, in new birth. This is what happens when two substances collide, when two spirits with different natures violently engage one another. Someone has to die.

Thankfully, one Spirit is lovingly giving the other the ability to die, and in so doing there may be a chance of resurrection. For without a life there can be no death, and without a death there can be no life. One cannot survive without the other.

By all accounts Paul should have died on the road to Damascus. Jesus should have released him from the privilege of air for what he'd done to so many women and children. But Paul was chosen. He was to be a missionary, a pastor, a pioneer, a Spirit-inspired theologian, and the most influential church planter our world has ever known—and this was ordained even before he was born.

One has to wonder though, what did Paul think about for those three days he was blind? Luke writes in the book of Acts, Paul would not eat or drink anything for those days. I tend to wonder if he was picturing the horrible things he had done. I tend to wonder if they were playing through his head like an old movie and if the background music was the echoing words of Jesus, "I will show you how much you must suffer for my Name."

I wonder what Paul prayed. I wonder if he prayed at all. I wonder if not eating had nothing to do with a spiritual act. I wonder if he didn't eat because he was sick to his stomach about who he had become. I wonder if Paul tried eating but threw it up in misery. I wonder if he had lost his ability to taste. I wonder if those were the most despairing three days of his entire life. I do not know. God knows.

I wonder sometimes if we should spend three days not eating or drinking after our first life-altering encounter with Jesus. I wonder sometimes why my sin doesn't take me to a place that physically makes my stomach hurt and takes the ability to taste from my mouth. Sometimes I think I would gladly take on three days of despair if it produced in me the same life of reckless devotion Paul had.

I don't think Paul quickly recovered from the experience on the road to Damascus. I think in his weaker moments, when he would see a family come to listen to one of his teachings in the temple, he battled flashbacks. I think Paul spent the rest of his life in a battle, and I think this battle against the man he used to be served him well in becoming the man Jesus always knew he would be.

Just as God handpicked David, the murdering, cheating, King of Israel, to be a man after His heart, God too picked Paul, a murdering, manipulative, self-absorbed, Pharisee of Pharisees, to write two-thirds of the New Testament. It is almost as if God chose Saul to become Paul and David to be David so no one could ever say they are too far away from His mercy.

## 13: the non-interest in résumé

I think God isn't interested in résumés because résumés look silly in heaven. To carry on the scenario of Dr. Bob standing before God being posed with a question, I would say if Dr. Bob pulled out a résumé with a cover letter, it would make the scene go from really big to really small and do so really fast.

Résumés speak of where we've been, what we've done, whom we've worked for, and for how long we've done so. The document's purpose is to impress someone who doesn't know us. It is a piece of paper telling of our pieces of experience. It is our occupational history, on glossy or matte paper—in our hand as a symbol of relational distance.

God is not interested in résumés because He knows us. No information on paper will help His knowledge. Also, God is not easily impressed. Résumés impress externally, and God is impressed internally.

God knows how much we love ourselves, our lists, our achievements, trophies, plaques, pats on the back, and how much these things take the place of our love for Him. God wants us to trust in His grace, not our résumés. He wants to be our reward. God wants us to stand before Him with our eternity at stake, trusting in one thing: our relationship to His promise.

In the New Testament, Saul turned Paul wrote a letter to the church that met in the city of Ephesus. In the second chapter of the letter he gives one of the most beautiful descriptions of the Gospel a person could read. I like to imagine a group of Jesus followers packed into someone's living room, anxiously waiting, when suddenly a man rushes through the door out of breath, saying, "I have Paul's letter!"

Then, I like to think the feeling in the room changes. People no longer feel tired. They find themselves anxious and at peace, excited, grateful, and prepared. Everyone settles into their seats, women and children on the floor, men standing along the walls.

The pastor carefully opens the letter and begins to read aloud the very words of the Spirit of God. A few minutes into the reading, these words fall from his mouth: "You were dead in your transgressions and sin, and you are by nature objects of wrath, but God, being rich in mercy, has made us alive with Christ even though we were dead in our trespasses." He goes on reading, "It is by grace you have been saved through faith. And it is not of your own doing; it is the gift of God, so that no one may boast."

I like to think at those words, this first century pastor has a hard time keeping it together. I like to think these words of Gospel rush through the room like the wind of life. I also like to think people in the first century didn't have a hard time thinking they had to work for their salvation.

Maybe it was easier for them because at that time there were not as many church buildings to raise money for and programs to volunteer for and not as many busy opportunities to get overwhelmed with. Maybe it's because they loved the Sabbath. Maybe it's because they were poor and simple and common people. Maybe it's because they had fathers. Maybe it's because they were oppressed, and following Jesus was freeing to them, and they hadn't yet found enough time to become obsessed with works-based righteousness. Maybe they believed, but then in turn did nothing about it. Maybe that's why the Spirit of God used James, the brother of Jesus, to write the Church another letter.

Anyhow, when I think about those verses in Ephesians chapter 2 and the picture it paints, I am hopeful and worried. Their story of grace and rescue in Paul's original letter is clear. Yet our stories of grace and rescue are littered with made up theologies, myths, and falsehood. Sometimes in our creative attempts to paint better pictures, we in turn clean up and culture the story. We devise well-intended, nice sounding doctrine, in order to make us feel better. Trouble is, the Gospel is not civilized. No matter how much we want it to be.

I can remember one story of the Gospel I heard someone say: Jesus was the captain of a lifeboat. Everyday He sailed His lifeboat around the calm ocean and after a few hours found people swimming. Then Jesus sailed over to them and threw out a lifesaver. The person wading in the water had a choice: grab the lifesaver—allowing Jesus to pull them in and sail to safety—or keep swimming. We were being asked to grab a floaty, and for the most part, I enjoyed the analogy and though it's not in the Bible, I believed it to be true.

It was not long though, before the floaty story was challenged by the stories I found in the New Testament. It seemed to me the apostles and the Spirit were asking me to hear another story. In this story, Jesus was again driving a lifeboat, but this time the ocean was filled with wind and waves. He's sailing a lot faster. In this story, Jesus' hair and clothes are wet, and there's no lifesaver in the boat to be thrown out. Then suddenly in this story, Jesus finds what He is looking for and abruptly leaves the wheel, takes off His shirt, and before the boat stops He dives into the water. He swims through the waves, down into the deep, to the one to be rescued, and finds them lifeless. And in a power only He could posses, He breathes life into their lungs, and carries them back to the boat.

In this story, the one to be rescued is not swimming around waiting, but rather lying dead on the ocean floor. In this story, Jesus is the Savior. Not a floaty. He throws Himself to someone who could not grab

Him unless they were brought to life. In this story, a better, more Biblical metaphor, Jesus is responsible for both the gift of life and the rescue from death.

The Gospel is not that we would grab a floaty. The Gospel is that we were brought to life in the midst of wind and waves, and then with every ounce of energy this new birth gives, we cling to the Savior. Though unintentional, the more we make of ourselves in the scenario, the less we make of Jesus. In turn, the more we make of Jesus, the less we make of ourselves.

In that first century house church I picture a child sitting in his mother's lap. During the reading of, "You are by nature objects of wrath, but God being rich in mercy," the mom puts her hand on the child's head and whispers, "See my child how much God loves us, and see child how great a hero Jesus is."

In the twenty-first century church I picture a well-dressed man, wearing expensive shoes, holding a briefcase. In his briefcase: a résumé and cover letter. In his heart: a speech, an arrogance, an entitlement—his trust in the wrong place.

In the first century church I picture men standing along the walls who have had their hearts brought to life by the fulfilled promise of God through Jesus.

In the twenty-first century church I picture men who believe in tradition more than they believe in a need for a Savior.

In college, I attended a church where half of the congregation was under 25. The other half of the congregation was over 60. This is not an overstatement; this was the truth of our gathering. One Sunday, our pastor stood up and spoke candidly to both sects of our church. He was a well-spoken man who had spent many years on the mission field and had a way of telling you terribly hard things that somehow landed in your heart as encouragement.

He began by asking the college aged people in the room to try and look at life through a different lens. He said he was proud of our passion, our activism, and our appeal to many outside the church. Then he walked to the edge of the stage and said, but be careful not to become what you have grown to hate.

He said, you may not realize this now, but you can become suffocated in tradition even at a young age. He said be careful. Do not become crusaders for dressing a certain way for church, for singing certain songs a certain way in church, and don't become married to a way of doing church and forsake the beauty of the history that has pointed you to the One who is the Way. He said when you think your method is the only method, and you sell yourselves to doing something exclusively this way or that, you have become just like previous generations—exactly what you hate. He said not to spend our energy preserving the wrong things. Preserve the truth of the Gospel, he said. Fight for the Gospel, not for songs and tee shirts.

Then he changed his cadence. In a more emotional tone he said, be careful, do not become like my generation. My generation fell into the same trap. We fought for the wrong things. We preserved too heavily a method rather than a message. At this point my pastor began to cry and to clap, but the clapping was in a tired and sarcastic sort of way. And through tears he said these haunting words, "I would like to extend a congratulations to my generation; congratulations friends, we kept our traditions, but we lost our children."

## 14: the interest in résumés

If you stand before God and depend whole-heartedly on the promise and work of Jesus, you will do well. God will be pleased with your position. He will respond gratefully. He may even tell you how satisfied He was in Jesus. And He may tell you stories you could never imagine. Time will stand still when you're with God. It will be the most alive you've ever felt, for you will exchange laughter with your Creator.

After a few moments of reminiscence and laughter God will catch His breath and say all right, wow, that's great. He might rub His eyes and take a deep breath to compose Himself.

Eventually, though, He will hold out His hand and say, "Well then, let's see it."

"See what?" you ask.

"The résumé."

"What do you mean, the résumé?"

Then you feel the Spirit pierce through the air and through your heart whispering, "Faith without works is dead. You believe God is One, you do well. Even the demons believe and shudder."

God is interested in our résumé because our résumé speaks of work and purpose. Résumés tell the story of our stewardship. How did we spend our borrowed time and borrowed money? Did we live the faith we claimed? What did we do with our lives? God is interested in résumés because in response to what Jesus accomplished, we are commissioned to give our lives away. We are to leave traces of our life and love all over the world. Résumés turn to testimony when held with the right heart. Résumés, when handed over in faith, attest to the relationship, not against it.

God is interested in résumés because His Son empowered us to be under the governing of a different kingdom. And in this kingdom everyone has the same responsibility: live in a place not their home and serve as ministers of reconciliation.

God wants to know if we had a faith that moved, a faith that transformed our actions. The résumé is our documented response, not our proof-of-purchase. The proof is the indwelling of the Holy Spirit. And the Holy Spirit empowers résumés.

James, the brother of Jesus, said speaking a language of blessing upon people in need but never being a blessing to people in need has grave consequences. He said a spoken word without actualization is a core disconnect from the confession. James said faith that does not actually show itself, is actually no faith at all. Without a working out in the external world, there is no proof of this alleged internal working. The shift in inward understanding must translate to a shift in external valuing. Jesus gave new birth for the sake of new worldview. People who believe in all Jesus has done have received a new birth, and this new birth is unleashed under a mandate—trust God, and love people.

It makes me nervous to speak of those particular words from James' letter without mentioning the song of salvation's baseline set in the Ephesians' letter. Ephesians 2 and James 2 are harmonizing for us the foundation in which faith is really faith. Faith is really faith when we understand it's available through the unmerited favor of God. We trust grace by using faith. He gives us faith to trust in grace.

Faith is faith when we trust that Jesus paid for our access to God. What we do now is a response to what's already been done. We work not to gain something, but rather work because everything has been gained. We must never think God is not pleased with us until we do a certain amount of good works. The résumé is handed over like a photo album is handed over after a wedding. Sure, it proves the wedding happened, but above all else, it brings the relationship such joy to remember the moments and the stories. Looking through a photo album is a celebration; you invite your friends over, pull out the teacups and take your time. The same is true with you, God and your résumé. It's a celebration of God's approval towards you, not a ticket for God's approval towards you.

The message of the Gospel of Jesus is to trust our good works are simply shadows of the cross. They never will, nor can they ever, overshadow the cross.

Paul, in his letter to the church at Philippi, says it this way, "Work out your salvation with fear and trembling." The Greek word for "work out" is where we get the English word gymnasium. It is a picture of sweating out the salvation process under a life of discipline. It is in the context of a daily routine. It is a picture of beating your body for a future glory.

The most important part of the verse though, is what it's not saying. Paul says, "Work out your salvation." He never says, "Work for your salvation."

Through faith in Jesus we are saved. In response, we work out our salvation. Our work is because of His work. Our agenda is to push forward His. All the good achievements in human history put together could never come close to accomplishing what one man did one weekend two thousand years ago. Reconciliation to God was given by the work of Jesus. The only natural response to Jesus is trusting in His work by living a life of work.

James writes to his audience with eerie sarcasm. He says belief in a foundational sense, namely, believing God is one, is not as impressive as some might think. Even the demons believe that, James says, and shudder at the thought. In the New Testament there are many moments when the demons have better theology than the disciples. Any time Jesus confronts someone with an evil spirit, the spirit immediately speaks out something in the vein of, "We know who you are Jesus, the Holy One of God." Demons have never had an issue of faith. They have always had and always will have an issue of works.

Demons exist to wage war against the purpose of God. Professing a foundational faith, or a working knowledge, in a God who is One—as demons do—followed by a life spent waging war against His purpose—as demons do—makes for a disease that finds no remedy in the court of God. Faith merely spoken, followed by a life not aligned with His purpose, is by all accounts dead. Faith that does not work is simply that—a faith that does not work. It has no life—no breath or movement. It is surely dead.

There is a harmony possible between faith and works. There is a place where faith and works mingle like lovers' souls.

This mingling is brilliantly portrayed in another of Paul's letters. To the church that met in Philippi, Paul wrote, "But whatever was to my profit I now consider loss for the sake of Christ. What is more I consider everything as loss compared to the surpassing greatness of knowing Christ Jesus my Lord, for whose sake I have lost all things. I consider them rubbish that I may be found in Him, not having a righteousness of my own that comes from the law, but that which is through faith in Christ, the righteousness that comes from God and is by faith. I want to know Christ and the power of His resurrection and the fellowship of sharing in His sufferings, becoming like Him in His death, and so, somehow, to attain to the resurrection from the dead."

These words come in the wake of Paul reading his own résumé. Though the people in Philippi were some of his dearest friends, many of them had a boasting problem. So Paul lists his achievements and dares someone to compare himself or herself to him. Because the truth is, his résumé would make us all want to put away our matte paper and cover letter. Paul had the lineage, the history, the scholastic, and even now the suffering. Yet he chooses to boast in one thing—the surpassing greatness of knowing Christ Jesus his Lord.

This is the sacred place where the music pieces itself together in the ears of God. This is a dance worthy song. This is the other headphone.

God wants us to have a brilliant résumé that inspires others, and a heart that yearns, "I want nothing more than to know Jesus and the power of His resurrection. I count my résumé as nothing compared to Him. My trophies are worthless in light of Him. If I have to choose between this list of achievements and Jesus, I choose Jesus, for He is the one I saw when I was raised from the dead and rescued in the ocean."

---

The late great singer/songwriter Rich Mullins once said in a concert, "The scary thing about God is He doesn't have a Plan B. God sent Jesus to the cross and the Church to the world. That is His plan, and it will work."

God wants to use the Church to meet the needs of the poor. God wants the Church to give their life away. God wants the church to make His invisible kingdom visible. God wants the Church to choose justice over comfort—the mission over maintenance. God wants the Church to be the greatest proof of His existence.

The people of God, inspired by the empowering of the Holy Spirit, released into the world for good works and disciple making, was what Jesus saw in His mind as He laid down His life. The Church should be the greatest résumé-carrying people group on earth. No one should outshine the people of God. No non-profit should out-serve the Church. But if someone were to point at the résumé of the Church and say, "Wow, you've done a lot," the Church should say, "This is nothing. My husband is far better."

God is first interested in our confession, then He's interested in our résumé. A résumé without a confession is dead, and a confession without a résumé is dead. An eternal harmony is found in the one who on the final Sunday is able to lay down a beaming résumé, that matches a beaming heart, that trusts in the blood of Jesus as the only cover letter that will ever gain God's approval.

## 15: the fringes

Understanding the meaning of grace gives needed perspective and inspiration to propel us into a life of works. After my second year at that all-boys R.A. summer camp, and my second conversation with my second counselor, I knew I wanted to work for Jesus for the rest of my life. I told the second counselor I never wanted a real job. I told him I wanted to work in a church, or in a ministry, or in a camp setting. I asked if he knew if this camp was hiring—specifically in the area of lifeguard.

I have come a long way in my understanding of what working for Jesus means. I realize now it can certainly be done anywhere, in any setting, under any title. Jesus gifts people in all sorts of fields of work for His glory. This was not always the way it was introduced to me when I was younger though. The concept of being called into ministry was portrayed as something heroic. It was sacred.

Ministry was reserved only for the most spiritual students. These students would receive extra prayer time at camp or youth nights at church. Guys and girls who felt God wanted them to be something else— a coach, or teacher, or artist, or engineer, or architect, or doctor, or designer, or anything else under the sun—had to sit and watch their special friends receive special treatment.

In most of those evening services or prayer sessions it was typical to hear someone quote Isaiah 6:8. The text reads, "Then I heard the voice of the Lord saying, 'Whom shall I send, and who will go for us?' and I said, 'Here am I! Send me.' These were the "Here am I! Send me," kids. I was one of them, but I had it all wrong. By hearing verse 8 alone, I pictured Isaiah standing on an altar or stage with mass crowds around him and when he proclaims with all his might, "Here am I! Send me," everyone in attendance applauds with a great roar and wipe tears from their eyes and whisper to each other just how great Isaiah is.

This verse in Isaiah is still used just about every time someone is called into ministry, whether it be youth ministry, vacation Bible school ministry, foreign missions ministry, or music ministry. In any sort of commission, into any sort of ministry, you find this verse. I never thought much of it until I got to college and Dr. Bob taught me about reading the Bible in context. I learned Bible verses don't belong to me. They belong to the first audience, in the context and social setting in which they were originally intended.

The story of Isaiah 6:8, is in a chapter with 12 other verses. Verses 1-7 paint one of the most terrifying and beautifully accurate pictures of God and His glory found in the Bible. Chapter 6 starts with the phrase, "In the year that King Uzziah died, I saw the Lord sitting upon a throne high and lifted up; and the train of His robe filled the temple." King Uzziah took the throne at age 16 and was the reigning King of Judah for 52 years.

He was faithful to God for most of his life until his pride led him to think he had the same privileges as the priests. So one day, he entered the Holy Temple to burn incense at the Lord's altar. Eighty priests opposed him, saying this duty was given by God's instruction for the descendants of Aaron, for those who had been consecrated.

Uzziah proceeded against their warning and received immediate punishment for his arrogance and contempt toward God. He was struck with leprosy before he left the Holy Temple and was required to spend the rest of his life in a separate house outside the city. The king had trespassed against a greater King and was now going to die a leper, alone, outside of his city.

This was a very well-known king and a very well-known story. Uzziah reigned for generations, but now he fell. For Isaiah to say, "In the year that King Uzziah died," would be like someone in our time starting a story by saying, "In the year the Twin Towers fell," or "In the year of Kennedy's assassination," or "In the year Pearl Harbor was attacked." Everyone had a reference point for this event. By speaking of Uzziah's death, Isaiah got everyone's attention.

Verses 2-7 tell of an Eternal King who is reigning from everlasting to everlasting. There's reference of the train of this King's robe filling the temple. This is significant because the length of the garment the king wore was a parallel to the length of his reign. Isaiah saw a King who had a train that filled the entire temple. In Hebrew this word "train" could even be translated as "hem," which means simply the edge of his train was being seen in the temple. Just the fringes of his garment were more than sufficient to fill up the place.

Isaiah goes on to speak of angels flying around the throne calling out to one another, "Holy, Holy, Holy is the Lord of Hosts. The whole earth is full of his glory!" Then the whole place starts to shake and fill with smoke and Isaiah cries out, "Woe is me! For I am ruined, I am a man of unclean lips and I live among a people of unclean lips and my eyes have seen the King, the Lord of Hosts."

Seeing God was not illegal in the Old Testament—it was just impossible. To see the God of the Covenant and live through it was something humans don't have the capacity for.

Isaiah says, "I am ruined," which could literally translate, "now I'm dead."

What happened next in the story is really important. In response to this vision of God something inside of Isaiah burst forth in confession.

The purity of God forced out the impurity of Isaiah. Somehow without provoke a confession is birthed.

Anytime angels appear to people in the Bible they typically speak two things. First, "Get up," and second, "Do not be afraid." Angels by nature impose a sense of fear. In this picture, Isaiah is faced with a King on a throne and countless angels crying out to one another in such loud voices they cause the ground to shake. Isaiah is terrified, trembling, broken. Before he is even asked a question he shouts out, "Okay I did it, I deserve death, I'm unclean, my lips are unclean, my people are unclean, and my eyes cannot handle this vision of You."

So here we find Isaiah facedown, waiting on death, when a seraph flies over to him, carrying a burning coal taken with tongs from the alter. The coal is placed on Isaiah's lips and the seraph says, "See, this has touched your lips, now your guilt is taken away and your sins atoned for."

The coal is placed where it's needed. Atonement assigned to the confession, healing given to brokenness. Cleansing covering the unclean.

Again we find Isaiah, probably facedown, probably with his lips on fire, probably still waiting on death when the voice of the Lord speaks. Through the smoke-filled, train-filled, glory-filled temple, a Holy voice booms, "Whom shall I send, and who will go for us?"

Isaiah eventually looks up, his lips still on fire. He's confused, he's hurt, and somehow he feels nearly dead and still much alive. "Whom shall I send, and who will go for us?" Isaiah has confessed, he has been cleansed, and he is now being given an opportunity for commission.

This verse, Isaiah 6:8, which baptized most commissioning services I was familiar with growing up, is set in the context of the most terrifying moment of Isaiah's life.

What bothers me is in all those settings, in all those commissioning services, I never saw—myself included—a horror in the face of the one being commissioned. The called one always looked so confident. So pretty and polished.

When Isaiah hears the voice of God speaking to him, I like to think he first realizes he is not dead. Then he realizes the grace extended to him and sees the option set before him as not much of an option. From somewhere deep within Isaiah's stomach, likely the same place that caused his first confession, he speaks out. But this time the confession is different. God says, "Whom shall I send, and who will go for us?" and the terrified, soon-to-be prophet looks around, wipes his mouth, stands to his feet, pushes back his hair, looks up and shouts, "I'm here. Will you send me? Can I go? I've seen who You are; I want to speak for You. Send me! Send me!"

My heart is moved every time someone reads the send me part. That a man would look at God and say with boldness, "Here am I! Send me," is powerful.

My fear is that taken out of the context of the whole story, verse 8 loses its power. When you don't see the terror, it's hard to believe in the confidence. When you don't see the risk, the reward is underwhelming.

When I was in college our church commissioned a friend of mine who just graduated and was following a call of God to go overseas and ride mountain bikes in the jungles of Africa trying to plant churches. During the service our pastor asked him to kneel down on stage. Then our Pastor asked some older men to come on stage and lay their hands on the young man. Then they prayed and they prayed and they prayed. Some of the men lifted their voices and their hands and pleaded with God on my friend's behalf. When my friend stood up, he had tears in his eyes, he was short of breath, and he looked horrible. He looked scared and overwhelmed and broken to his core. He never looked better.

Somewhere in that prayer time it seemed he was confronted with a vision of a glorious God, the reality of his sinful self, the beauty of an unwarranted forgiveness, and the grace    of a heavy invitation: confession, cleansing, commissioning. The order of calling.

What happened to me when I felt called was simple. I thought I would get a job working at a camp or church or somewhere and I would be nice for the rest of my life. I had no concept of the Kingdom of God or of long-suffering and heartache. I wasn't yet afraid.

No one told me it was going to be hard. There have been times when life showed me more about ministry than ministers showed me about ministry. I never realized there was a chance you could fail and you could fall into sin and that you should watch your life closely. I had no idea I was so prone to pride and lust and being judgmental and that I had authority issues. I never realized the prayer of my life would come from a line in an old hymn that reads, "Prone to wander Lord I feel it, Prone to leave the God I love, here's my heart Lord take and seal it, seal it for Thy courts above."

## 16: the calling

As backward as it sounds I wish someone would have sat me down and told me the hard stuff. The wonderful 60-year-old missionary couple I had seen at R.A. camp looked so happy and peaceful and looked like they had given their life to Jesus and received a joyous gift because of it.

Looking back, I bet they had long seasons of sorrow, many stories of hurt, and years of trusting this invisible God to pull them through heartache. I bet they lost friends, had family conflict, and saw people pass without ever coming to know the Light of the Gospel. We were teenagers. We couldn't handle those stories.

I think when missionaries share and students respond to a call to missions there should be an immediate after-call meeting. In this meeting the missionary should tell the called students of the pain, the sacrifice, the agony, the long hours and little reward. And then just before the missionaries have talked the called kids out of it, they exhale, and with a smile and confidence in their eyes they say, "But students, it's worth it; Jesus is so worth it."

Maybe at commissioning services we could say to each participant, welcome to the family, and then hand them a biography of a missionary. Maybe this would show very clearly that throughout history many great men and women of faith have given their lives to a people group or a nation who turned out to be obstinate, stiff-necked and proud. At the age of 28, the Auca Indians of Ecuador killed Jim Elliott before he could tell any of them the story of Jesus. William Carey, the man known as the "Father of Modern Missions," lost his first and second wife and his 5-year-old son while on the mission field in India. Maybe if we looked at historical missions we would see the beauty of   contemporary missions. David Livingston, Hudson Taylor, Adoniram Judson, and Corrie ten Boom would be very helpful.  It would be helpful if modern missions remembered that two hundred years ago when "the called out ones" followed a calling it meant getting prayed for at church, kissing your family, getting on a boat, going to another nation, sharing the Gospel, and dying.

If we listen closely we can hear the God of the Old and New Testament, the martyrs, and the missionaries who have gone before speaking to us.  They ask us to live well in our Saturday, to join them in the fellowship of suffering, to come die for the sake of the Gospel, to see this life as but vapor.  They ask us not to be handcuffed by our comfort, busyness, and possessions.  There's an ever-open invitation to leave our SUVs and storage units behind and find our deepest joy.

If I'm honest, I'll tell you, I think short-term church mission trips have it all wrong.  We come home with slideshows and souvenirs.  We tell the church we did something with their money.   We say we'll go again next year.  Oh, and we mention the people who have not yet heard of Jesus—because, of course, they too are in the slideshow.

It may not be as malicious as I make it sound, and forgive me if I'm being harsh, but I think this is true.  I have seen many people, though, find a burden birthed on the mission field and I rejoice in that, because I know those 10 days overseas will give them Godly perspective for the rest of their lives.  But, truth is, I have been a part of the mission trip stories that were monopolized by the little inconveniences. Sleeping on the floor, eating weird food and taking cold showers have dominated many mission trip share nights.  We want church people to be proud of us.  We want

Jesus to be proud of us. We want to be in fellowship with the suffering. It's just our definition of suffering is so weak and we have idolized it. We have been misinformed. We love comfort. We love showing off our passports. We have good intentions. We just do not have the right perspective. We have yet to learn that missionaries don't carry cameras: Tourists do.

## 17: the slideshow mission trips

When I was 15, I went to Johannesburg, South Africa for two weeks on a short-term mission trip. In the eight months prior I raised money, studied language and culture, and convinced myself I was going to Africa to lead people to Jesus. Truth is, I just wanted to go to Africa. I thought it would be cool and impressive. And I was obligated. I was a student who felt called to overseas mission work, and had been ambitious enough to say it out loud. So when Africa was mentioned, I knew I had to go. I'm grateful for the sense of obligation I felt, because Africa changed my life.

Our mission team put on a play in market areas, neighborhoods, squatter camps, and soccer fields. We performed seven or eight times a day. After our play someone from our team would share his or her testimony through a translator. Then they would invite people into a prayer of salvation. This was called "casting out the net."

The drama we performed was a 20-minute sketch following the life of two people: The Journeyman and The Miracle Man. In the first scene, a group of people wearing black clothes, white gloves and blindfolds are going through the motions of life: working, eating, sleeping, working, eating, sleeping.

Somehow in the routine the Journeyman has his blindfold knocked off. He looks around and for the first time sees the world. He's fascinated by the possibilities, the questions, the unknown. If we are not here to simply work, eat, and sleep, then what are we here for?

And thus, the Journeyman begins his journey.

During his exploring he is befriended by a man wearing a white shirt and a warm smile. The man in the white shirt tries to tell Journeyman the meaning of life, but after a few sentences they're interrupted by the first group the Journeyman meets on his journey: The people of greed.

The people of greed proudly proclaim the reason we live is possessions, wealth, prosperity. These men and women are driven and dark—a deceitful people who manipulate others to get what they want. In the middle of this scene a struggle breaks out over a bag of money. The Journeyman is immediately overtaken by his newfound greed and kills a woman. He puts his hands around her neck, takes her to the ground, chokes her, and stands up arrogantly flaunting a bag of money.

As he runs around showing the crowd his reward he realizes something terrible. He starts to shake so violently he drops the moneybag. His gloves have changed. They are no longer white—they've changed to red.

The Journeyman kicks the moneybag away and tries to pull the red gloves off but they won't budge. They are just as much a part of him now as his very nature. He is terrified by what this could mean and is remorseful for what he's done. Finding life's purpose has been replaced by a passion to get these red gloves off.

The music changes, a group of people rush toward the Journeyman carrying weapons and yell that the gloves don't matter, what matters is power. With power comes authority and with authority you can accomplish anything. The power people try to beat the gloves off him. When they're unable, they decide to beat the Journeyman instead. The people of power leave the Journeyman bleeding and alone, lying on the ground still plagued by his red gloves.

Eventually the Journeyman tries to pick himself up. As he's doing so he feels he's being helped. He looks back and sees the man in the white shirt. The man in the white shirt reaches for the gloves but the Journeyman pushes him away, hides his hands, and shakes his head in denial. The man in the white shirt doesn't budge. He isn't afraid or ashamed. He reaches again for the gloves.

Their scene is interrupted by loud music and chaos. A group called the party girls barge in and say who cares about the gloves, just drink and medicate your life away. Of course this doesn't work either. Following their scene the people of intellect try to take the gloves off by finding the answers in books. But again, everything fails. No one has the ability to take the gloves off. The Journeyman is hopeless.

The drama is performed to music and no actual spoken words. Someone who speaks the language of the people records the narrator's voice into the music. It is a fast moving sketch and the American missionary actors are dressed up to play the parts. The stage was usually dirt and the audience ranged from 30 to 300 people, of all ages.

Every group fails to take the gloves off the Journeyman. He's miserable. He's frustrated. The Journeyman is defeated and alone when a few people from each group charge him and reveal his hands are red because he is a murderer. The sentence for his crime is death but before they kill him, he deserves to be beaten. During the beating the man in the white shirt rushes in and throws himself on the Journeyman. The mob throws aside the Journeyman and the man in the white shirt, called the "Miracle Man," tells them, "Take me instead."

The Journeyman wakes up to the sound of the Miracle Man being beaten and even crucified in his place. He tries to intervene but it's too late. The mob throws him to the ground again. There is nothing he can do except watch and weep.

Every time we performed the drama the crowd became very silent and drawn in by the sacrifice of Miracle Man. Some would get mad and shout out, "This is not fair! This is not justice!" After the Miracle Man was pronounced dead, he was laid on the ground and the actors formed a circle around him symbolizing a tomb.

The music turns from dark, to quiet, to silence, to confusing, to loud. The actors look around wildly and when the music is at its crescendo there is an explosion. All the actors fall to the ground and the Miracle Man jumps up from the tomb. The first thing he does is run to the Journey Man and without conversation, Miracle Man picks up Journey Man, grabs his hands, rips off the red gloves and throws them to the ground.

As this is happening the rest of the actors go into the same movements of the opening scene, work, eat, sleep, repeat. The Journeyman asks Miracle Man what he can do now. Miracle Man points to the routine people and says go show them your hands.

The performance ends with Journeyman running from person to person showing his clean hands and pointing toward the risen Miracle Man. Some are intrigued and come to the Miracle Man and some turn away and continue to go through the motions.

The crowd always enjoyed our performance and always stayed to hear the American teenage missionary share their story. Once the net was cast and the connection was made between Miracle Man and Jesus, we went into the crowd with translators and asked people if they wanted to believe.

I probably prayed with 100 people over those 10 days.

They prayed to Miracle Man at the market, at the ball field, in the squatter camp. After the prayers, we got on an air-conditioned bus, sang worship songs, and left them with their only knowledge of Jesus coming from a skit. There were no local churches to connect them to, no one to disciple them, and no Bible to give. A 20-minute drama and a prayer was what we offered. None of us were going to give the rest of our lives.

When I came home from that trip, you know what I talked about? I talked about eating alligator at an expensive African restaurant and seeing a real lion on our half-day safari trip. I talked about taking cold showers and being sacrificial because I don't like to eat vegetables but I had to for those days. I even had a slide show to prove my faithfulness.

In college, our Missions professor told a story about a man who spent 40 years in Africa. He said even after all those years this missionary still felt like an American. He said he would have given 10 years of his life for just one hour in the mind of an African. When asked if his ministry in Africa was successful he responded, "Success in ministry is measured by the names of individuals." Then he began to tell stories of people by name who had changed, been discipled, and even become church planters. He told of people who now had a faith of their own.

It kills me to say, but I don't remember one person's name from that trip to Africa. Not one. I don't even stay in contact with the Americans who went on the trip with me. It is something I bring up occasionally but I have no passion to go back or stay in touch or sell my possessions and buy Bibles and send them their direction. And I bet I could say the same is true for the 30 other people who went on the trip with me. Odds are some of those 30 are currently not walking with the Miracle Man in their own lives.

The next summer I went on another trip with the same organization and we performed the same drama but this time it was in Venezuela. Same story in the aftermath. No continued passion for Venezuela. No sacrificial love for the people there, simply stories of food, showers, and sleeping situations, and of course, a slideshow.

The only thing I remember from Venezuela is in one poor community, a 70-year-old blind woman came out of her home to listen to what we were doing. Someone on our team thought it would be a good idea to pray for her healing. So we gathered around her and started praying. Then someone on our team thought we should do what Jesus did, you know, take some mud and wipe it on her eyes.

So, 16 teenagers and 4 adults, all dressed in face paint, wind pants, and solid colors, smeared mud into the eyes of an elderly woman in a poor neighborhood in South America. We prayed for ten minutes, then someone got water and washed the mud off. By this time 50 people or so had gathered around to see what was going on.

When we patted dry her eyes she was still blind. Our prayers had not worked. All we accomplished was getting a 70-year-old woman's face dirty, and her blouse wet. She was gracious, as was the community, but nothing could hide the awkwardness of the situation.

As we got on the bus and drove away, I thought surely I was the reason the woman was not healed. The whole time we were standing around her I could not get past the fact we rubbed mud in her eyes. I was thinking too much and praying too little. I was doubting and daydreaming and wondering if we were foolish to mimic Jesus in this way. To make up for it, I prayed this beautiful elderly lady would receive her sight when all the face-painted Americans were gone and could take no credit for it. The Lord knew 10 years later we wouldn't remember her name. The Lord knew we couldn't be trusted with that sort of miracle on our résumé.

## 18: the meantime

I haven't been on an overseas mission trip since. Sometimes I think of those people I prayed with in Africa and Venezuela. I hope God sent them a real missionary—someone who planted a church in their neighborhood, someone who bet their life on the cause—someone who didn't show up with a camera.

I hope the Africans and Venezuelans remember the short-term face-painted Americans who told them a story of One who took a beating in their place, took the grave in their stead, and rose again to take away the stains we have plagued ourselves with. I pray they make it through the meantime.

The meantime is Saturday. The meantime is nothing. The meantime is when we sit and wait in silence. This should come as no surprise. God's people have always been asked to wait. The entire Old Testament is one story of waiting. It's told by many stories and by many men, of course, but in the end it's one story, about One man, waited for by one people.

In Genesis 12, God speaks to Abraham and says, "Abraham, I love you, I'm going to bless you and make you the father of many nations. Everything is about to change; the foundation under your feet is about to shift." But, God says, in order for this shift to happen, Abraham has to leave his household, his worldview and everything he knows about other gods. He has to follow an unknown God. Abraham has to learn his new name.

Gods were not usually this intriguing or interested in individuals. Gods in Abraham's time were powerful and frustrated. To appease them you offered things—many things—the best of things. In the most extraordinary acts of worship, you would offer your first-born child in hopes of gaining the gods' approval.

The God who spoke to Abraham promised a child. He delivered on His promise. A miracle child was born and they named him Isaac, which means laughter—because everyone laughed at the idea of his birth—because his parents were so old.

Just a few years into their relationship God says, "Abraham I want you to offer Isaac to me." God asked for an offering. Abraham was used to this, he had seen it many times in his culture and he was just getting to know this God so he was willing to oblige. Who knows what kind of wrath might be poured out if he disobeyed?

Abraham takes Isaac up to a mountain, builds an altar, lays the child of the promise on the rocks, and as he lifts his knife to slay his son this God speaks again. He tells Abraham to stop. He says, "Look, there is a ram caught in the thicket. Go and kill the ram I have provided as an offering instead."

This God provided. This God used years and years of Abraham's life to tell him a story he would never forget. Abraham sat in the meantime for years and fought through poor choices and inadequacies in order to get to that moment. God was leading Abraham. He was telling him a story, calling him to more.

The story of God and Isaac and Abraham on the mountain has something to do with Abraham but everything to do with God. The faith it took to go through the process of potentially sacrificing your son to this unknown God is remarkable, but it's not the point of the story, it's not the point of the meantime. The point is when the knife was raised, when everything was at stake, God intervened with provision.

God led Abraham to that mountain, on that morning, in that moment, to speak to him an eternal truth that would shape the entire nation of Israel and the people of God forever. And the truth was: Abraham, I am not like the others.

## 19: the Savior in the dirt

There are many pictures of long-suffering in the Bible—many stories of a God who is not like the others. In John chapter 11, Lazarus, the brother of Mary and Martha, dear friends of Jesus, gets sick. Jesus loved this family. Throughout His life He spent many days and nights with them. When Lazarus gets sick, the family sends word to Jesus. Jesus gets the news, waits three days, then makes the journey to see them.

When Jesus arrived in Bethany, Lazarus had been dead and in the tomb for four days. Before Jesus makes it to the house of Mary and Martha, they hear He is in town and Martha goes out to meet Him. Mary stays in the house.

Martha speaks to Jesus very faithfully, theologically even.

She tells him, "Whatever your will, Lord, it will come to pass. I know Lazarus will be raised in the final resurrection."

"Martha, I am the final resurrection. Those who believe in me will live even though they die."

Martha wipes away tears, "Yes, Lord; I believe You are the Christ, the promised One, the Son of God come into the world."

Jesus embraces Martha and says, "Let's go look for Mary."

Mary is still inside, not ready to talk.

There is another story of Mary and Martha in the Bible. Jesus is teaching at their house and Mary is sitting at the feet of Jesus listening while her sister Martha serves the guests. Martha asks Jesus to tell Mary to help with serving. Jesus responds to Martha, "Oh Martha, I can see you are very troubled, but Mary has chosen what is better."

Thinking of that story reminds me that Mary and Jesus had a close friendship. And Mary's frustrated with her friend Jesus. She can't believe He didn't come home to heal her brother. She can't believe He took so long. Mary knew better than most the power and legitimacy of Jesus. She knew He could have stopped what happened. She knew He had healing in His hands.

The Bible says when Mary sees Jesus she breaks down. She runs to Him, falls at His feet and cries, "Lord, if you were here, my brother would not have died."

The Bible goes on to say when Jesus saw her weeping—and all the Jews who had come with her also weeping—He was deeply moved and greatly troubled in His spirit. So much so the people cried out, "See how He loved him!"

The shortest verse in the Bible may also be the most profound: "Jesus wept."

Can you picture it? Jesus, the Author of Life, the Beginning, the End, the future and current King of all things, the Word become flesh, the Savior of the world, weeping in the dirt over the death of His friend.

## 20: the end of the story

If you've been around death you know how it goes: someone dies, people get together to remember. Usually this gathering takes a while—family and friends show up slowly, over a couple days. Each time a loved one walks through the door they smile and wave, trying to hide the grief in their eyes. But before long you're all in the kitchen, someone pulled out the pictures and everyone's weeping again.

With each memory told, the emptiness returns. Emotions come and go, stories are told and re-told. Waves of peace and grief relentlessly pour over you. The deceased must not be forgotten. It's a terrible process. But it's part of the meantime.

After crying with Mary and Martha, Jesus goes to the tomb. And again, just as before, He weeps. He looks at the people gathered at the gravesite and is deeply moved. He knew many of them. He grew up with some of them. And they were in mourning, which meant Jesus was in mourning.

What fascinates me is Jesus doesn't go to the tomb just to visit and mourn with the others. He goes to raise Lazarus from the dead. Jesus knows where the story is headed. He knows everyone present is about to see something they have never seen in their lives—a physical resurrection of a man four days dead. Yet, when Jesus shows up, He doesn't tell everyone to stop crying. He doesn't run in and yell, "Hey everyone, relax, give me a minute and you'll have no reason to mourn." No. Jesus takes His time. He embraces His friends. He weeps—real tears, from a place of real sorrow. His posture of grief speaks even before His words. Jesus doesn't seem to mind the process. He's not afraid of the pain.

Somewhere in the midst of the sorrow, Jesus composes Himself, looks to the tomb, and asks that the stone be rolled away. Martha interrupts, "Lazarus has been dead four days; there will be a terrible smell if we roll away the stone."

Jesus looks at Martha and says, "Martha, my dear, I've told you, if you believe, you will see the glory of God."

The stone is rolled away, and Martha's right, the odor comes pouring forth. Men and women cover their faces and turn away—the heat and the smell too much to bear.

Jesus, not shaken, looks up and says, "Father, I thank you for hearing Me. I know You always hear Me, but I'm saying this for the benefit of those who are here, that they may believe You sent Me."

Then Jesus fixes His eyes on the tomb and in a loud voice says, "Lazarus, come out!" Dr. Bob always said Jesus had to specify "Lazarus" because if Jesus just said, "Come out," everyone buried in that cave would have walked out.

After what felt like eternity, Lazarus came stumbling out wrapped in linen. Four days dead, yet now he lives. Everyone's amazed. Jesus tells them plainly, "Take the grave clothes off him."

## 21: the grave clothes

I went to college to study the Bible. My professors liked me because I wasn't waist deep in presupposition. I wasn't indoctrinated. Yet. At least that's what they told me.

They liked me because I wouldn't raise my hand in class and tell them what they were saying didn't match up with what my legalistic grandmother taught me. I didn't have a legalistic grandmother. Many of my classmates did. That, or they were governed by the ever-present voice of a previous youth minister.

My teachers didn't have to beat me down to build me up. I was already down. I knew I didn't know. I knew I was behind. I was excited to be quiet and learn. Sure, I attended church growing up, and started to read the Bible on my own in Junior High, but I was nowhere near the level of Bible knowledge my classmates had. I knew the major themes of the Bible but not the details. I learned the devil is not in the details, God is.

Most days I sat in class mesmerized by the knowledge available in this one sacred book. And I felt overwhelmed. They respected that.

Though my church history wasn't comparable to the people next to me in class, my life history certainly was. I didn't have clothes of piety to pull off; I had clothes from the grave clinging to my back. I had an internal authority problem, a lust problem, an addictive personality problem, a trusting problem, and an array of other problems burnt into my heart that needed correcting.

Grave clothes are the worst. They are who you used to be, ever wanting to come out of your closet and remind you of your insignificance. Grave clothes accuse. Grave clothes bid you return to death. Grave clothes are only at home in the tomb.

Jesus wore grave clothes for a day and a half. He was killed and buried and wrapped in linen. When His first followers visited His tomb on beloved Sunday, they found no body, only linen. Jesus left His grave clothes behind. He knew there was no use for them. He conquered death and found no reason to be reminded of what the tomb was like.

This death to life picture dominates the Christian narrative. Even the terminology given to salvation by Jesus is "to be born again." It's as if our first birth was into death, into a fallen world where everything's fractured, all of humanity broken, and from the moment of this first breath we are moving toward dying, toward tasting death itself. And for as long as we are in death, the grave clothes are collected, wrapping themselves around us like vines.

But then the miracle happens. Jesus jumps out of the lifeboat, swims to the bottom of the ocean, breaks into our grave, and breathes life into our death. He rescues and a new life is given. And while we're sitting on the deck of the lifeboat trying to catch our breath Jesus turns and says, "Take off your grave clothes."

The second birth is a birth into life. From the first breath of our second birth we are ever living. The old is gone. The new is come. Death is dead. Life is alive. Problem is, we still have choices and most of us can't be trusted. Something in us longs to go back to the ocean floor. The poison is somehow provocative. It's absurd really, but it can't be denied. There is death in us revolting against the life in us. It's shameful to say, but it's true: sometimes we would rather be dead. The grave clothes have appeal. The tomb is ever calling and its song is seductive.

In college I felt it. I would be sitting in class learning the truth of the Gospel and hear voices whispering to me that this was a joke, that I was a joke. I would wake up and look in my closet and see nothing but grave clothes. Some days the grave would creep in under my door and other days it would walk right up and punch me in the stomach. I could be in a prayer meeting and see someone wearing a "True Love Waits" ring and be reminded of my life in the grave. It was relentless. It was at war with me. There was no place I was safe. I can feel it even still.

You have to be aggressive with grave clothes. You have to fight back. If Lazarus had walked around for the rest of his life saying, "I would rather be dead," then the miracle would have been in vain. But Jesus does nothing in vain. Jesus brings people to life so they can live. He doesn't rescue us to just let us drown again.

## 22: the storm of the summer

I took summer school between my junior and senior year of college. I needed six credits to stay on track to graduate the following May. That summer my campus was empty, my dorm room was empty, my relationships were empty, but in the solitude I found life.

I was taking two classes—Spanish class, taught by the school's soccer coach, and golf class, taught by the school's baseball coach. They wore sweat pants to class and usually let us out early. Most of my evenings were spent studying vocabulary words while putting golf balls across my living room.

That summer I had a job working the front desk at the campus gym. It's a small workout space. I was the only employee from 6:00 A.M to noon. Since I didn't have much of a social life, I would go to bed early and get up early. Some days when I wanted to spice things up, I'd go to Wal-Mart and walk around the book section whistling. I'd stay there for a while hoping to see someone I knew. I never did. So, eventually I'd leave with a few on-sale fiction books. I remember reading a lot that summer. Not just Wal-Mart fiction but all sorts of books. And I listened to a lot of music. And I had a routine.

Every morning I'd get up before the sun and make coffee. Then I'd drive to the gym, unlock the door, open the gate, turn on the lights and the music, and sit at the front desk for three hours before I'd see another person. Sometimes I would fold a towel or two, if I felt like it.

On Thursdays a group of men in their 60's would be waiting for me at the door before six. They came in to play racquetball and talk about the way things used to be. They wore short shorts and headbands and had their own racquets and goggles and opinions. I loved those old men.

Ronald Reagan died that summer. One morning I came in, turned on the television at the gym and every station was talking about how Ronald Reagan died. I didn't know much about him outside of the Berlin Wall so I was intrigued. I put a tall chair on a treadmill, propped my feet up and sat there for hours watching the nation mourn. The news talked about what kind of president Reagan was and all he'd accomplished. Ronald Reagan was an old man when he was president—older even than the men who came in to play racquetball. I remember thinking, I hope I'm able to play racquetball or be president when I'm their age.

That summer was the first time I read a whole book in one sitting. The book was *The Great Divorce* by C.S. Lewis. It's a short book but not a short story, if that makes any sense. There's one scene in the story where two old college roommates are talking. One is an angel and the other is not. The angel roommate says, "Do you remember in college when we wrote papers about the Bible?" The other roommate says, "Sure I do." Then the angel roommate says, "Well, was there ever a time when you thought all the stuff in the Bible was actually going to come true?"

It seemed so basic to hear, but something about the phrase "Have you ever thought it's actually going to come true" really bothered me. I remember putting down *The Great Divorce* and looking around the empty recreation center. Somehow the room looked different—emptier than usual. Somehow at eight in the morning C.S. Lewis scared me. I thought I was in the twilight zone. I wanted to walk outside to see if there were still other people on Earth. I wanted to call my roommates and ask if they were angels. I wanted to ask them if they had ever thought about the Bible coming true.

The thought is so simple but so powerful, "Have you ever thought about all the stuff you've read in the Bible coming true one day?"

I hit golf balls and studied vocabulary words differently that afternoon. I kept looking up wondering if the sky was going to crack. At first it was scary. I wasn't ready for Jesus to return. I had too much to do. I wanted to get old and play racquetball and run for president. I wanted to shoot under 100 on the golf course. I wanted to graduate. I wanted to get married. I wanted control. But if there's one thing you can't control, it's when the sky will open.

In East Texas clouds grow dark quickly. One minute you're resting on a towel sunbathing, the next you're running for cover because heaven is falling. Floods happen in a flash. They don't always, but they can. There are other times though, when the sky grows gray in the distance, when slowly the darkness tracks toward you and there is nothing you can do about it. You watch across a parking lot as rain takes over inch-by-inch, effortlessly swallowing cars and concrete.

One night that summer one of those storms rolled in—slow and steady, methodically thundering. I was alone and could hear the rumbling and stirring outside my apartment. As the sounds grew more intense I went out and sat on my steps. For more than an hour I witnessed the power of God barrel toward me. I sat in silence, physically feeling the weather.

Eventually the electricity went out and everything went dark. The only time I could see was when lightning lit up the sky. But I wasn't afraid. I felt safe, like my Father was with me. I felt like I was the only person in the world that night, and God was speaking to me, though He never said a word. He didn't have to. As the storm drew near, so did He.

Somewhere in the midst of chaos a new kind of peace came over me. I started to feel a growing calm in my soul. I didn't care about my golf game anymore, or about running for president, or playing racquetball at 70. I didn't care about finding a girl and getting married or getting a job, or making money, or buying stuff. I didn't care about anything but knowing the One behind this storm. I didn't care about anything but this relationship, this silent conversation. I closed my eyes and breathed deeply.

The air felt like His tangible presence and I wanted to drink it in. I could have sat there forever. I felt contentment in my bones. I told Jesus He could come back right then if He wanted to. I told Him I would be completely okay with that. I sat right there on those steps, and whispered, "Come back. Come back. Come back already."

## 23: the mission of God

I'll never forget the night on those steps. I've had moments since then that flirted with the feeling I had, but nothing has been quite as pure. When you sincerely look to the sky and for the first time in your life ask Jesus to come back, it's hard to forget. But telling Jesus you're tired of Saturday is no easy task. You think it's illegal or something. It's not.

I had a professor in college who was also the pastor of the local church I served in. His name was Dane. Everyone called him Dane. In class you raised your hand and said, "Dane, I have a question." He was one of those guys who was easy to be on a first name basis with. My freshman year of college I took an Intro to Ministry class from him. He walked in ten minutes late and said, "My name is Dane. You can call me Dane. I've been on the mission field in India and Africa for as long as I can remember so I'm not accustomed to wearing a watch. If I'm late, I'm sorry, give me ten minutes, I'll be here." I loved him at hello. I took every class I could from Dane. Missions and Church Planting was my minor and Dane taught the majority of the Missions and Church Planting classes, so he played a major role in shaping my life.

Dane was the best storyteller. In our missions class we would always ask him to tell us stories about demons. He faced a lot of spiritual resistance in Africa and we wanted to know all about it. We ate that stuff up. Not every class has the ability to make you afraid to go the bathroom by yourself.

Dane told us one story about being in a market buying a few things when outside the tent he heard yelling. Then a man Dane had never seen before walked in and started pointing at him and screaming, "Missionary! Missionary! Missionary!"

The man ran toward Dane and Dane said the only thing he could think to do was yell back, "In Jesus' name I command you to leave me alone." And it worked. The guy fell to the ground convulsing. So Dane paid for his fruit and walked home. I remember thinking, "That's old school." And I remember thinking, I'm glad nothing like that happened to me when I was in Africa. I would have stood there and gotten beat up with bananas in my hand.

Dane taught me to see ministry as people. He said, just like the other African missionary said, success in ministry was measured by the names of individuals. I believed him. Dane taught me how to take seriously the call to reach the world. He taught me what the word indigenous meant. On Tuesdays I had Dr. Bob's class and Dane's class back to back. Most Tuesdays, after their classes, I'd walk around campus with my hands in my pockets and my heart on fire wondering what I was going to do with God's grace in my life and God's mission in the world. Those two men were obsessed with the mission of God. And their obsession burned a hole in my chest.

I'll never forget one Tuesday toward the end of the semester, Dr. Bob looked out at our hermeneutics class and said, "I want to say thank you for taking this class. I want to thank you for taking the Bible seriously and for taking God's mission seriously."

Then Dr. Bob started to cry. He grabbed his Bible off his desk, held it up with one hand and said, "Not everyone takes this book seriously anymore. Not everyone is putting in the hard work." He paused, caught his breath and continued, "Everyone wants a shortcut." Then he raised his voice and said, "Well, there are no shortcuts with the Bible. If you're going to preach it, you have to know it; you have to put in the work. You have to sit with the book and beg the Spirit to help you, and it's hard work. And I thank God that you're putting in the work. And trust me, I've begged the Spirit to help you."

Then Dr. Bob put down his Bible, wiped his eyes, smiled and said, "And I thank God every day most of you in here are weirdos. Because you weirdos are going to be able to reach people me in my suit and tie will never be able to reach. Keep being who you are, keep putting in the work, keep telling the story, and trust that God will fulfill His mission through you."

It was about that time I was trying to decide what I was going to do with my life. It felt really good to walk around campus that day and think about what Dr. Bob said. It's encouraging to be told, "Keep being who you are." I'm not sure I was the weirdest person in class, but in many ways I felt different and unable to fit in the traditional church setting.

The church I was currently working in was formal and traditional, but Dane was the pastor so I was okay with it. For a while I was the interim worship leader there and was considering staying on after graduation. Toward the end of my senior year, I turned in a formal résumé and it was brought before a committee who was going to make a decision on whether or not I could come on staff full-time.

The meeting was on a Sunday afternoon. I came in Sunday night to talk to Dane about how it went. He told me the committee loved me and would be honored to have me become their Worship Pastor. I smiled, thinking I had the job. Then Dane said, "Josh, I told them I didn't think you should get the job. I told them I wasn't going to hire you. I told them you didn't need to work here."

I didn't understand. I immediately felt defensive and hurt. Having your pastor tell you he didn't want to work with you can take your breath away.

I finally asked why. Why don't you want to hire me? Dane looked around the hallway as if to see if anyone was coming. When it seemed all was clear he looked at me with an intensity I wasn't sure I'd seen before and said, "Josh, you don't want to work here. This is not what God has for you. If you took this job it would be a good thing, a comfortable thing. But Josh, the last thing you want is a good thing. You need to leave East Texas and attempt something great. Go plant a church, go start a movement, go tell the story as only you can. Josh, I can't keep you here. God has a bigger mission for you. Trust me. He has something great for you. And working here is not it."

Sometimes you hear things in your head and sometimes you hear things in your soul. This was one of those soul moments. It felt like Dane took on the role of the Holy Spirit for two minutes and spoke directly to my heart. His words were water to a place I didn't know was thirsty. It was comparable to the feeling I had while sitting on that ping-pong table with the counselor at the all-boys youth camp. I felt unleashed. I felt commissioned. I felt like I could run fast. If I had had long hair, I would have driven home with the windows down letting it blow all over my face. I felt in some strange way I had been given permission to go and participate in a story and mission far greater than anything I had ever known.

## 24: the great white hope

One day in class, Dane told us a story about when he first got to Africa. He said he showed up thinking he was the "Great White Hope." He said he arrived with a lot to teach to these pastors and a lot to say about missions.

The first thing Dane did was call a meeting of all the pastors in the area. They would start at 10:00 A.M. on Saturday. He arrived at 9:00 A.M. to prepare the tent and go over his notes. When time came to start, the room was empty. He went outside and looked around and there was no one in sight. He waited inside, growing anxious and frustrated as each minute passed. How could they stand him up? How could they be late? He was important, he had a lot to teach these people. Didn't they understand?

At 1:00 P.M. the oldest pastor in the area showed up. For the next five hours, men trickled in one after another. And at 6:00 P.M. the final pastor walked through the door, making the attendance complete. Dane stood up, flew through his material, and within thirty minutes was finished. He told everyone to leave and if he ever called a meeting again they'd better be on time. The local pastors left, heads down, notebooks in hand, without saying a word. The room emptied until the only one left was the oldest pastor who arrived first.

The elder pastor came to Dane, put his hand on his shoulder and said, "Missionary, thank you for coming and teaching us. You have good things to say and much I hope to understand. But there is something you must understand too, something about Africa." The elder pastor said, "Missionary, these men you dismissed walked for days to get here. And if on their way they found someone who needed to talk or needed help, they helped them or talked with them. These pastors were more on time for this meeting than any meetings we've ever had. You should not feel angry. You should feel honored. But you must understand this: in the West, time matters most, but in Africa, people matter most. The Church is the people, not the time."

Dane said he sat on the ground, put his face in his hands and wept. His pride melted with each word this man spoke to him. He repented of thinking he was the Great White Hope. He repented of loving himself more than the pastors.

That conversation changed the way Dane viewed the world. He was shown what it means to contextualize, what it means to slow down, and most importantly, he was shown that God's mission is the same everywhere, but it plays out differently amongst different cultures. Dane said the Great White Hope died in the tent that day and what resurrected was a man not wanting to teach, but wanting to learn. Dane said you should never believe anything is yours. All ministry is God's. Everything is God's.

Dane told us in missions, the goal is to become a leader who trains leaders and as quickly as possible begins to come up with an exit strategy. He said the best pastors in Africa are not Americans, but Africans; the best churches are led by pastors from the area. The quicker you train and get out of the way, the better. The less you bring in from the West, the better—the more indigenous, the better.

Dane said he taught this concept of exit strategy some years later in Africa to American missionaries. Dane said one missionary stood up and yelled, "How could you say that, what I am doing here is my ministry, this church is my church. I'll never leave, I could never trust my church to them!" Within the month, Dane had that missionary taken off the field. Nothing is yours, Dane told him, everything is God's.

I remembered these stories when I left the church I wanted to work in. I remembered thinking whatever I did, I had to do with open hands. I couldn't cling to it and call it mine. Nothing was mine, not money, not relationships, not even the mission.

## 25: the skit and the temple

God grew on me in high school. He progressively revealed Himself—I progressively fell in love.

My home church was small, so it wasn't long before I stumbled into leadership. As soon as I could play four chords on the guitar and strum in rhythm, I was asked to lead worship. Those fine people pushed me to lead and invited me to start things.

My freshman year of high school I started a group called CSU, the "Christian Student Union." We met once a week at 7:00 A.M. in the school's auditorium. We sang songs and had an adult come in and lead a devotional. My high school was small and God wasn't taboo and our group wasn't persecuted. We were mostly the cool kids, if you want to know the truth of it.

Things went smoothly for our weekly meetings. We led the "See You At The Pole" gathering as well. See You At The Pole is a once-a-year nationwide prayer event. Out of 220 students in our high school, 80 showed up to pray with us at the flagpole.

I bring this up because I think in some settings, God is appealing, and East Texas is one of those settings. In East Texas if you ask someone where he or she goes to church they usually have an answer, or at least some small association with some church they can mention. And in a basic sense it's not offensive—they are not offended. Where I live now, in Pullman, WA, if you ask someone where he or she goes to church they may say something like, "Church? Why would I go to church? Do I seem like the kind of person who needs to go to church?" They don't take offense, or respond defensively, it's just in some way, they don't understand where the question comes from.

Cultural Christianity is what I'm getting at. It is something you do, rather than who you are. It's God in the meantime, but not really God in the meantime. It's poison really.

Here's what I mean: the greatest gift of the meantime, of Saturday nothing, is God. He's the One we have now and the One we are waiting on—to have fully later. He's the joy in the midst of sorrow, the hope relentlessly reminding us that things won't always be this way. God is the better forever. And to know the One responsible for the creation and reconciliation of all things brings peace. And to have a relationship with the one true God through the work of Jesus is enough to make the waiting bearable. A Saturday filled with nothing spent with God is still a beautiful Saturday.

But the issue is not God; the issue is in what we're waiting on. Many of us are waiting on the return of Jesus, sure. Many of us may even look up to the sky each day, God knows, and whisper, "Come back." But many others are waiting on shortsighted relationships or jobs or money or turning 21 so they can drink beer or their big break or their great idea or whatever. God in the meantime is glorious, as long as you're waiting on the right God.

I've lost many friends over Jesus. Not because of a conflict, but because our connection was Jesus and one day they decided Jesus was no longer interesting. They got bored. They turned to other things, to shortsighted gods. They moved in with their boyfriend or girlfriend. They started playing video games or believing philosophy books or smoking pot or having sex. Their life found temporary meaning elsewhere.

They got tired of waiting. Their God was too small to begin with. This story is all too common, all too troubling. We should never get bored with Jesus. We should never find ourselves fulfilled elsewhere. But it happens. Everyday it happens.

When we follow Jesus we have to understand He's not a means to an end. He's not what we do while we wait for the job or the relationship or the big move to the new city. Jesus is not a friend you hang out with until you get real friends or find someone to call you beautiful. He's not the comfort you find when your bank account is empty and the one you abandon when the bank account is full. He's not a puppet. He's not interested in charity. He doesn't need us.

I've lived in a world where Jesus was portrayed as a passive-aggressive wimp who begs for our attention, then once we give Him a minute of our time He gets all aggressive and wants all our time and the secrets of our heart.

I even remember seeing a skit at church camp where Jesus is at some guy's house on a Friday night and they are hanging out, doing whatever people do when they hang out with Jesus. All is well, so it seems. Then the phone rings. It's an invitation to a party. Jesus gets whiny and begs the guy to stay and keep playing Scrabble. Jesus pulls out a deck of cards and Monopoly to provide options. The guy is not interested. He lies and manipulates and says he's not going to be gone long and he's going to be good while he's at the party.

"Come on Jesus, what's the big deal, I'll be right back," he demands. Jesus complains again and begs him to stay, even pulling on his shirt. Eventually the guy heads for the door and Jesus follows still pleading his case. Then in a dramatic moment the guy turns around, grabs Jesus's hands and nails Him to a metaphorical cross to keep Him in the house while he goes to the party. The skit ends with the guy walking out the door and Jesus hanging on a cross in his living room.

The book of Colossians says Jesus made everything in the world that has ever been made. It even goes on to say everything made was done so for Jesus, through Jesus, and that it all holds together by the words of Jesus' mouth. So, Jesus can hold the world together by the word of His mouth, but He can't keep a high school kid from beating Him up in a living room.

There's a story in the Bible where Jesus shows up to the temple and finds the religious people have made a deal with the money handlers. They are using God for profit and making it difficult for the poor to access a place of prayer. Jesus sees this and runs through the temple in a holy rage, flipping over tables, yelling at them that they have committed a great sin. Then He finds a whip and starts hitting people. Jesus forces these men to leave. In an aggressively loving act, He clears the temple.

I'm guessing there were a lot of men in the temple selling animals and making profit. I'm guessing this wasn't pleasant and the people getting their tables flipped over weren't happy. But the story doesn't say one of the men walked over to Jesus, took away His whip, beat Him with it, and sent Him and the disciples on their way. The story doesn't say Jesus got punched in the nose and went home crying, holding His face. The story goes: Jesus walked into the temple, grabbed a whip, started hitting people, flipping over tables, opening animal pens, throwing money on the ground, and nobody stopped Him. Nobody took His whip away. Nobody punched Him in the nose. Everybody ran.

Jesus said, "My Father's house is to be a house of prayer and you've turned it into a den of robbers." Zeal for His Father's house consumed Him. He fought for the poor and brought the nearness of God back to a holy place. He made a mess. He made things right.

We don't nail Jesus back to the cross when we go to parties and we couldn't beat up Jesus if He was in our living room. And Jesus wouldn't beg us to stay. He wouldn't moan and groan and pace the room and pull out board games and worry and pull on our shirt. He would sit on the couch, keep eating popcorn, and let us go, because Jesus doesn't need company. But He wants company. So He would invite us to stay. He'd look at us with a warmth and welcome we've never known and say, "Are you sure you don't want to stay?" And if we didn't stay, we would be missing out on Life.

The only thing true about that skit is most of us would rather go to a party than spend an evening with Jesus.

## 26: the opposition

Just as much as there is a Hope who restores through the meantime, so there is an enemy who destroys. We don't talk much about the opposition. Maybe it's because of the images that flood our mind when we think of evil. We can already see the man in the expensive suit with sweat on his face reaching to touch our forehead yelling, "In the Name of Jesus..."

That guy makes us nervous. As he should. But what shouldn't make us nervous is a conversation about a dark darkness and a bright light. For there is darkness, a deep dark darkness that opposes all that is light. And there is a Name that when called upon in the dark brings light—a Name that changes the darkest of things.

I have friends named Amy and Matt. They have three boys. Their youngest, Luke, is 6 years old and like me at that age, he's afraid of the dark. Amy told me one night she went in to Luke's bed, laid down with him, and told him whenever he gets scared to start saying the name of Jesus over and over again. They practiced it together right there. Luke is 6 years old and he's being taught to speak "Jesus" when he feels afraid.

I can picture Luke a couple nights later, he's had too much sugar and can't fall asleep—he's lying in bed holding the covers to his chin—looking up into the darkness. He starts to feel afraid. He hears noises. He hears the silence. Then he remembers what his mom and dad said, and he tries it, he starts whispering the name Jesus. And I can picture Jesus drawing near, sitting on the edge of his bed, running His hand over Luke's forehead, providing protection and peace. I think Jesus likes when Luke calls His name.

I have another friend named Kurt. He and I were roommates in college. He fell in love with a girl far more beautiful than he is good-looking. Her name is Jen. We were in the same friend group with Jen and on weekends we would go to the lake together. Kurt would get up early those days and go to the gym to do pushups and curls. We'd pick him up on the way out of town and as soon as we got to the lake he'd take his shirt off and go stand by Jen, hoping his arms still looked big. It worked.

Kurt eventually convinced Jen to marry him. I stayed over at their house a few months ago and Kurt woke me up by throwing two dogs in my bed, moving my blanket off me with a shotgun, and saying, "Get up, coffee's ready." In Texas, that wake up call is a high honor. I appreciated the gesture.

Kurt and I had a lot of the same issues in college. We both had the thought life of a sailor and the scars of poor choices. We had mutual baggage, a mutual calling, and a mutual love for guitar. We would stay up late and play our guitars and dream of the type of men we would turn out to be. It helped us bond and feel normal.

On one of the darker days of my life, I locked myself in my room, laid face down on my bed, and hoped to wake up in another time and city. Kurt knew what was going on and the sin I was living in, so he laid on the floor outside my room, sang annoying songs, and kicked my door relentlessly until I opened it. Then he forced me into his truck, drove me to the Outback Steakhouse, bought me an expensive steak and made me talk out my issues. Kurt was easy to confess to. He was a guy who had a lot of grave clothes to get out of in his own life.

While we were at Outback and I was eating steak and crying, I told Kurt it felt like my chest was caving in. I told him I was hearing voices. I told him not to think I was crazy and not to tell any of the Christians at our school. Christians at our school were perfect and didn't hear voices so I didn't want it out there that I was hearing voices and wasn't perfect. Kurt shook his head and looked at me with eerie understanding.

Then he told me when he was younger he heard voices. He said he's always had a strange connection with the unseen. He told me there were mornings when he would be sitting in a deer stand hunting at 5:00 A.M. and he would see things and hear things. He said the voices condemned him, told him he was worthless, told him God could never use him. Kurt said one morning when the voices were at their worst he heard, "You know you can end all this right now, you can put that shotgun in your mouth and end all this."

If it weren't my friend Kurt telling me this story, I would have had a hard time believing it. But Kurt is far from crazy. He usually told the truth, and his moments of exaggeration were more endearing than dangerous. So, I believed him, and I asked him what he did. He told me, right there in the steakhouse, the only thing that would make the voices go away was the name of Jesus. He said he tried praying and closing his eyes and putting down his gun but the voices only got worse. So he said he started saying the name Jesus, crying out to Jesus, asking Jesus to take the voices away, and quickly the voices slowed down, and before long came to a complete stop.

I've never heard voices that aggressive. And I've only dabbled with moments when I felt as though I was better off dead. Honestly, I don't think there is anything magical about the name Jesus. But I think what Luke, and Kurt, and even Dane in the market in Africa, had in common was a heart in need, a gut level honesty, and a faith in the right Jesus—Jesus who conquered the grave, not Jesus who gets beat up by high school students.

Jesus who walked out of the grave two thousand years ago is the One who has the power to defeat the opposition. He can be trusted. His name spoken in faith can move spiritual mountains and silence the opposition. Luke couldn't defeat the darkness, Kurt couldn't silence the voices, Dane couldn't stop the attacker, but Jesus could. So they called out to Jesus, believing He would come, and He did.

I once read a book by Frederick Buechner and in it he says when you tell someone your name you give them power. Because now, if they see you in the street and call out your name you will stop, turn and look, and even respond. I thought about Jesus when I read that, because Jesus has told us His name, and in so doing He's given us the power to call on it, and the good news is, every time Jesus hears His name called, He responds.

## 27: the road and the magician

I spent the first year after college living in a car with a magician. In a way, it was taking Dane's advice and looking for something great. My friend Drew was the magician and he had been influenced by Dane the same way I had. We took a video camera, a map, and a dream to 35 of America's 50 states. Along the way we performed in coffee shops, local churches, and a lot of random venues now that I think about it.

If you had a couch we could sleep on and a crowd we could speak to, we were willing to come. I did the music. Drew did the magic. We stayed busy week after week and always seemed to make enough money to keep going. Our expenses were low. We ate trail mix and beef jerky as meals. And in the 12 months on the road with Drew, we never once paid for a place to sleep. Couches, guest bedrooms and Wal-Mart parking lots are free. So, we frequented them. We carried a tent and a mattress with us. Everywhere was home.

Drew and I didn't have a church or a pastor for a year. We drove 6-8 hours a day. We had time without content. Our friend Jason traveled with us for a while. He had a unique ability to entertain for long stretches of time—partially because he drank 300 energy drinks on our trip. On days when Jason wasn't up for entertaining, we put a small computer on the dashboard and watched episodes of Smallville. Jason and Superman kept us sane.

Sometimes we read the Bible out loud, or we'd read other books out loud, or we'd sing songs out loud and judge each other's voices. Our only real tradition was prayer every morning before we started the car. We asked God to provide. And He did. Everyday He did.

When we ran out of Smallville, stories, and songs, we started listening to sermons. Our favorite preacher was a guy named Matt Chandler who pastors a church in Texas. I had four of his sermons on CD, so we listened to those until we had them memorized. Then Drew learned how to download sermons from their church website and put it on an iPod. In a matter of minutes we went from four sermons to 100 sermons. Matt Chandler became our pastor.

We would listen to one after another until we had made our way through entire books of the Bible. He preached like a house on fire and we loved it. Sometimes Jason would have to go to the bathroom because of all those energy drinks but we wouldn't stop because we wanted to keep listening.

I'm the kind of guy who loves knowledge. It's a way I connect with God. It's a way He connects with me. When some spiritual truth makes its way into my head, it's not long until it makes its way into my heart. I remember once listening to a guy named Bob Kauflin talk about leading worship. He said leading worship was not just singing a few fast songs before "the meat of the service." Bob Kauflin said leading worship was essential work; that it was "putting the truth of the Gospel on the congregation's lips and praying it seeps down into their heart." That's what Matt Chandler's preaching was for us. It was the Gospel in our heads, seeping into our hearts.

I remember one night it was late and we needed to get gas. We pulled into a station but none of us could open the door and get out. Matt Chandler was telling a story and we sat there in that gas station parking lot for 20 minutes until he finished. He said when he was in college he had a friend named Kim. Kim was a single mom who Matt and his friends became close with. Matt invited Kim to a concert. Well, really it was a "True Love Waits" rally, but there was a concert at the beginning. The guy preaching got up after the music and spoke about sex using a rose as an illustration. The preacher passed the rose around the auditorium inviting 1,000 students to touch it, smell it, look at its beauty.

After 30 minutes or so the preacher asked for the rose back. Some kid brought up the flower and it looked nothing like before. It was tattered and torn and petals were missing. The rose was broken to its core. Then the preacher held it up for all to see and said, "Now who would want this dirty rose?" Matt Chandler said a few weeks later his friend Kim got thrown out of a moving car by some drunk guy. When Matt went to see Kim in the hospital she was asleep. He waited for hours until she woke up. When Kim woke up she looked at Matt and the first thing she said was, "Matt, am I a dirty rose?"

Jason, Drew, and I sat in a truck at a gas station in the middle of nowhere Oklahoma fighting back the tears. Matt Chandler said if he could go back in time he would go back to that rally and when the preacher asked, "Now who would want this rose?" he would stand up and yell, "Jesus wants the rose!" Matt Chandler said the very basis of the Christian faith is that Jesus wants the rose.

That story changed the way Drew, Jason, and I saw people. It may sound strange, but it did. We became more intentional after hearing about Kim and the rose. Matt Chandler told us people have souls. He said they aren't just machines who do things for us, but they are people, made in the image of God, and they have a soul. Realizing people have souls is essential to living well in the meantime—because the realization is half the battle. And if a spiritual truth makes its way into your head, it has a chance to make its way into your heart.

## 28: the waitress and the radio

Matt Chandler's story of Kim and the rose reminded Drew, Jason, and me of a spiritual emphasis week we had in college. Dane brought in a preacher who graduated from our school 10 years prior, and he preached on campus every night for a week. This preacher was different than the others. He told us stories about interactions he had at truck stops and all-night diners. This preacher said one of his favorite things to do was to ask a waitress, "What is the biggest need in your life right now?"

Sometimes the waitresses gave huge elaborate answers and sometimes they would say something practical. One lady said she just wanted a pack of good cigarettes. This preacher asked her what her favorite cigarettes were and she told him. Then he asked when her lunch break was. She told him. Then this preacher went and bought a carton of this lady's favorite cigarettes and brought them to her on her lunch break.

The preacher said the lady was blown away. She asked him what he did for a living and why he was buying her a carton of cigarettes. The preacher at our spiritual emphasis week told the lady he was a pastor from another city and he bought her cigarettes to meet her need and to tell her God loves her. The lady said, "Sir, it's a shame you're from another city, because I wouldn't mind going to your church."

Then the preacher told us another story of a lady who said her biggest need was going to the dentist. She said she had a terrible tooth-ache and didn't have the money to afford a check up. The preacher asked her, if he paid for her to go to the dentist, would she? She said yes. He went to the nearest phone book, found a dentist, made the appointment and called the waitress back.

A few weeks later he got a call from the dentist office saying they had seen the waitress and it turned out she had cysts on her gums and when they tested them they found she was in the beginning stages of mouth cancer. The receptionist told the preacher they found the cancer in time and could get it all but needed to know who was going to pay for the oral surgery. The preacher said, "You go tell your surgeon the Light of the world is going to pay for this." The receptionist asked for credit card numbers and the rest of the story.

A couple weeks later the preacher got another call. It was the same receptionist. She told him the surgeries were successful and they were able to get all the cancer and there was no sign of it coming back. The waitress was fine—everything was finished. But before she hung up, the receptionist said, "I told my surgeon what you said and I told him your story, and he told me to tell you he's the Light of the world too, and there will be no charge for the operation."

I think that preacher told us those stories because he had been in our seat. He went to the same college we were in and he knew how easy it was to live a safe, boring Christian life. He knew if he asked us our issues we would say stuff like praying too much or loving too much or volun-teering too much. He knew we were lame. That preacher never bragged on himself in these stories. There wasn't a hint of pride to be found in his tone. He actually made much of God in the stories, and essentially told us nice Christian kids that people have souls. He was trying to teach us to be a blessing. He was asking us to open our eyes.

That preacher said he didn't know whether or not that lady be-came a believer, but he knows he felt God ask him to help, so he helped—

not to get her saved, but because he was saved. He said obedience is what matters. He said life is ongoing obedience to the promptings of God. He said he hoped we would steward our gifts well and be found faithful to follow God's promptings. He said he was afraid if we kept ignoring God's promptings, God would quit prompting. He didn't want that for us.

The reason I liked that preacher so much was because that year I spent a lot of time at the Waffle House. The Waffle House is not officially a truck stop, but if there were a vote for unofficial truck stops, the Waffle House would pass, no doubt. The people who worked there looked tired—like they were coming off their second job, running on a mix of hard knocks, caffeine, and nicotine. I liked talking to them though, even more than I liked talking to people at Christian college. The people at the Waffle House had a depth in their eyes that made you wonder what they had been through, or what they were going through, or what they had seen.

One night I was there a couple weeks after spiritual emphasis week and I thought I would try what that preacher tried. My waitress' name was Tracy and I asked her, "Tracy, what is the biggest need in your life?"

She said, "Honey, now that's a question. Let me fill this coffee, and get back to you."

Through the course of my waffles, Tracy and I became friends. She told me about her daughter and her granddaughter. She told me they had been living with her for the last year. She told me about growing up as a single mom herself and knowing how hard it is. She told me she had seen a lot in her life.

She said, "Josh, I haven't always looked liked this, there was a time when I was a beautiful woman."

"I don't know what you're talking about Tracy, you're still a beautiful woman."

She smiled, "Thank you, kind sir, I'm flattered."

Tracy kept working and stopping and talking periodically. I didn't bother her again with my question. If she didn't want to answer I was okay with that. Pressure is never a good idea. As I was paying for my food and gathering my things to leave, Tracy walked over and said, "A radio in my car. The biggest need in my life would be to have a working radio in my car." She said, "My home life is hectic, my grandbaby cries a lot. My work life is hectic and that Waffle House jukebox is lousy." She was right about the jukebox. Anytime I wanted to hear something, I'd put four quarters in and play Steve Miller's "The Joker,", four times in a row. It was the only good song available.

Tracy said she loved music and wanted to listen to something as she drove. Her radio broke a few months back and the silence was killing her. I told her I was thankful she shared with me. I said no one should have to drive around in silence if they don't want to.

A couple days later, I went back to the Waffle House at midnight with four friends and a car stereo. We walked in and asked Tracy if we could have her car keys. She asked what for? I held up a box with a new car stereo inside. Tracy froze. She started laughing and crying and walked around the counter and gave me and the guys with me a hug. Then she told the Waffle House we bought her a car stereo because hers was broken. Everyone in the restaurant cheered. We installed the radio and I left a Steve Miller Band Greatest Hits CD in the driver seat.

The next time I went to the Waffle House, Tracy sat down at my table, handed me waffles and said, "This one's on the house." We talked about God as The Joker played in the background. Tracy said she always thought God was love but the people who followed God weren't loving. She said she'd made mistakes, said her life was a mess, and essentially she was a dirty rose. I told her God loved her. Really loved her. And that God could be trusted. And that He was good. And I told her if Jesus had to pick between hanging out with me and hanging out with her, he would probably pick her. I told her Jesus really enjoyed people who had tough times and crazy stories and who liked music. I told her we bought her a stereo because we loved Jesus, and we wanted her to know Jesus didn't want her driving around without a stereo.

It sounds strange really, me telling a lady Jesus cared about her stereo, but it wasn't strange to her at all. Tracy said she hadn't felt cared for in years, said she couldn't remember the last time someone bought her a gift. For her, the stereo was more than a stereo: It was an invitation to a better story. It was God telling her she's not dirty. It was one soul serving another.

## 29: the cigarettes and Sam

I met Sam at a truck stop at two in the morning. I was eating. Sam was counting change. I was there with my friend Leslie. Sam was there with his backpack. We were the only three customers in the restaurant. Sam started the conversation by saying, "Hey son, could I borrow I cigarette?"

I replied, "Sorry, sir, I don't smoke."

"I'm sorry," he said, "I thought I saw smoke coming from your table."

Sam was homeless. He owned a backpack and a beard. That was it. He counted pennies on his table and didn't even have enough for a cup of coffee. Leslie and I, remembering the preacher from spiritual emphasis week, thought we should buy Sam some cigarettes. I turned back and asked, "What kind of cigarettes do you smoke?"

He said, "I don't know," and he held up a Ziploc bag of cigarette butts he'd collected off the road. He had smoked 30 cigarette butts.

Leslie ran to the convenient store next door and bought Sam a carton of cigarettes. I sat down at Sam's table and asked if he was hungry and wanted breakfast. We ate together and he smoked. I couldn't believe how quickly he devoured his food and cigarette. He couldn't believe we would buy him food and cigarettes. And he couldn't believe we were willing to sit at his table.

Sam told us he was headed to Nacogdoches to meet a friend. Nacogdoches was about an hour and a half from where we were sitting. I had a car and no plans for the next few hours so we gave Sam a ride. As we drove, he kept smoking and talking. It was three in the morning and the sky was dark and cold, the stars brighter than usual, the air crisp and piercing.

Eventually Sam asked me what I did for a living. I told him I worked in a church. Sam took a drag of his cigarette, looked out the window and said, "So you really believe there is a God, huh?"

"Sam, I really do," I said.

"You believe this God created all those stars in the sky?" he pointed out the window.

"I really do."

Sam kept looking out the window, "Well, if there is a God, and if He is powerful enough to create those stars I sleep under every night, then I tell you what: that God doesn't want to talk to me, and I don't want to talk to Him."

Sam told me he lied to people. Everyday he lied to people. He said he asked for money for food, then he'd go buy alcohol instead. Sam told me he was an alcoholic.

He said, "Five years ago my wife died. Josh, I fell into such a deep depression I couldn't get out of bed in the morning. I drank and drank and drank. I lost my job, my house, my everything."

"I wasn't always like this," he said almost to remind himself.

"I wasn't always like this, you know, people won't even look me in the eye when they pass, but I wasn't always like this."

Sam started shaking his head and began to cry, "My wife would kill me if she knew what I'd become. Oh God, she would kill me."

The Nacogdoches city limit sign arrived in the headlights at four in the morning. We took Sam to Wal-Mart and filled his backpack with food. It was awkward walking around Wal-Mart with a homeless man—

even if it was four in the morning. We care far too much of what others think. We forget so quickly people have souls.

I told Sam God wanted to talk to him. I told Sam there is no one in the world better to talk to than Jesus. I told Sam anytime he felt alone or miserable or craving alcohol or nicotine to ask Jesus to help him. I told him Jesus loved helping people with addiction. I told him all he had to do was call out His name.

Sam said, "All I have to do is call out His name?"

"Yeah Sam, you have to call out His name, and you have to let Him help you, and you have to be honest with Him, and you have to trust Him." I told Sam if anyone could be trusted, it was Jesus.

We dropped Sam off in a parking lot surrounded by woods. He said his friend had a camp in the woods and that he could find it from the parking lot. Leslie and I gave Sam a hug and watched him walk toward the woods. It was cold that morning. We could see his breath rising over his head as he walked away. We could see him pull his jacket around him tight. Sam was a big man, his steps slow and deliberate. He stopped right before he entered the darkness of the woods, turned on a flashlight, pointed it to the sky and called back to us, "So you really think there is a God and He really created all those stars and He really wants to talk to me?"

"We really do, Sam," Leslie and I yelled back.

Once Sam was gone we got back in my car, turned up the heater and prayed for Sam before we left the parking lot. Then we rode silently for a while. We watched, as the sky grew bright, the darkness submitting to the light. The stars faded and the outline of clouds became visible. The air started to warm. We listened to music and rolled the windows down every few miles to keep us awake. Then Leslie started to cry. She said she couldn't believe how selfish she was. She couldn't believe how much stuff she owned. She said she was ashamed of her life. I understood. On every level I agreed. I said me too.

When I got to my apartment, it was 6:30 in the morning. I made a pot of coffee and grabbed my Bible and turned it to Luke chapter 6. It's where Luke gives his account of the Sermon on the Mount. Luke never personally spent time with Jesus but wrote what Jesus did based on eyewitnesses. Luke had a heart for the poor—a huge heart for the poor. No one talked about and loved the poor more than Luke. I read Luke chapter 6 out loud. And as the words came out of my mouth they fell heavy on my heart. "Blessed are the poor, for theirs is the kingdom of heaven."

In Matthew chapter 5 this same verse reads, "Blessed are the poor in spirit, for theirs is the kingdom of heaven," but in Luke, the spirit part is left out.

I think God wanted Luke to leave it out on purpose. I think every word of the Bible is on purpose. I think God is good at writing. Even if it is through fallen men, God is still good at writing and every word He uses is intentional. The entire Bible is one big breath of God. One deep exhale we're to breathe in for the entirety of our Saturday.

Luke and Matthew are saying something more similar than we realize. Luke records Jesus' words as, "You're blessed if you're poor, and the kingdom of heaven is yours." The fewer possessions you have on earth the less likely you are to get strangled by this earth. And in Matthew's case, if you're poor in spirit it's much the same. When you're broke spiritually and broke financially, the Kingdom is close to you. The God of rescue is more accessible. You're not as likely a prisoner. You're near. You're blessed.

As I looked at the Bible, the words came off the page and floated around the room putting me in a trance. I may have just been tired. Either way, I was picturing Sam and Leslie and how their stories were much the same. Sam was near because he was broke in his wallet and Leslie was near because she was broke in her heart.

God was offering the kingdom to the broken. Jesus was offering His inheritance to those in poverty.

## 30: the absence of God

Where I went to elementary school, roll was called every day. Our teacher stood up and called out each student's name and if you were there you would say, "Here." If you weren't there and the teacher called your name, you would not say here, and your name hung in the silence. The teacher usually said your name again, louder this time, and looked up from her list to make sure you weren't asleep or dead.

Sometimes another kid in class would call out, "Not here," for the one who was absent. And sometimes another kid, who was friends with the absent kid, would tell the teacher just why Absent Kid was absent. "He's sick," or "His mom came and got him at lunch," or "He's getting braces today."

I remember the first time I read the quote, "God is dead." The audacity of it impressed me. It's like the teacher called out God's name in class and there was silence. So, Friedrich Nietzsche picks his head up and says, "God. Oh, He's not here. He's dead."

Other kids in class surely called back, "No, He's not dead; He's in such in such place doing such and such thing." But nonetheless, the seeds were planted, the damage done. Friedrich's claim certainly swayed people.

The silence of God is terribly frustrating. Can you imagine the frustration Pontius Pilate felt when he asked Jesus, "What is truth?" And

Jesus just stood there. Beat up and bloodied, Jesus stood there, silent as the dead. Frederich Buechner says when you are the Truth and someone asks you, "What is truth?" there is nothing left to do but stand there. The silence is the answer. Jesus responded profoundly by not responding at all. Without saying a word Jesus said, "Pilate, Truth is; you're looking at it."

The trouble with God is He doesn't have to respond when the teacher calls roll. He doesn't have to defend Himself to Nietzsche or affirm the other kids in class who say, "God's in Africa." But nonetheless the question of God's presence is an important one—for if God is absent, it's a terrible thing.

On the cross right before Jesus died, God was absent in a sense. He was there, because He can't not be there, but He turned away. And Jesus could hardly bear it. And if Jesus could hardly bear it, how are we to bear it? How are we to live in our dark days of doubt and how are we to battle the voices, the opposition, and the meantime?

Sam thought God was absent. Tracy thought God was present but unhappy with her. My mom thought God saved her life. Nietzsche thought God was dead. Kurt thought God kept him from putting a gun in his mouth. Dr. Bob and Dane thought God was unstoppable in His mission. And Pilate thought God couldn't answer a simple question. The stories fall all over. God's reputation is life-giving to some, irrelevant to others.

Pain seems to be God's problem. The question He gets most often is, "How could you?" Presence seems to be God's solution. In short: God doesn't give answers, He gives Himself—because if He is not enough, no answer in the world would suffice. The meantime is full of questions. Saturday nothing is one big question after another. We must come to see the point of life is not answers. Answers are dead. God is not.

## 31: the death of just

There was a worship leader in the charismatic church I frequented growing up named Lee. He was a large black man who wore shirts that looked
like they were painted on to his arms. Lee had a rough background, lots
of grave clothes. Once at church he was asked to share a part of his testimony. Lee stood up and said he used to get in fights a lot. He said every
weekend he would find himself at Sonic somehow getting into a fight.
Lee said he had a lot of enemies.

When Lee started following Jesus he quit going to Sonic and
fighting and started reading the Bible and saying words like "blessed" and
"anointed" and "glory." God was changing Lee's life and it was evident to
those around him. But it didn't change the fact that Lee had huge arms, a
gold tooth, and lots of enemies.

One Friday night Lee went to Sonic to get food. He ordered his
burger and cherry-limeade and turned to walk back to his truck. As he
was walking he got blindsided by a fist from the past. Lee put his hand on
his cheek to feel for blood and looked back at the guy who hit him. Then
Lee said, "Jesus tells me in the Bible if I get hit by my enemy on one cheek
to turn and let him hit me on the other cheek. But Jesus doesn't tell me
what to do after that. So the way I see it, you've got one more chance to
knock me out, then who knows what's gonna happen."

Lee said the guy walked away. I would have walked away too.

I had a hard time worshipping God when Lee led the singing. I couldn't quit looking at his huge arms banging the keyboard and his one gold tooth that showed if he opened his mouth just right. Lee said Christians should take the word coincidence out of their vocabulary. He said he got hit in the face that night at Sonic because God wanted to test his faith. He said if you love God, you'll be tested.

I don't know how I feel about coincidence. I think it sort of exists, sort of doesn't. I think I don't have an opinion. I know the phrase "divine appointment" makes me feel funny. Usually when someone tells me a story involving a "divine appointment" my eye starts to twitch.

They ask, "Why is your eye twitching?"

"Twitching?" I say, "No, it's fine. Please carry on with your story, don't mind me."

All I know is a lot has happened in my life I could never take credit for. A lot has worked out really well and could even be called divine. I've been blessed, anointed maybe, and even had moments of wanting to shout glory. Things come together and things fall apart. That's all I know. Maybe it's all an act of God, maybe it's an act of will, maybe it's an act of the opposition, or maybe it's God's hand over the fallen world allowing things to fall and land as they may. Or maybe God has removed His hand from certain things, certain people. Who knows? God knows.

Trusting God with the trivial is important though. Understanding that nothing is meaningless and people have souls helps you put to death the most meaningless word in the English language. The word "just." Whether God is in heaven writing in an appointment book with the word "divine" engraved on it, I don't know. Whether each decision I make is an act of me or an act of Him, I don't know. I know I'll be held accountable to God for what I do and I know God's accountable to Himself for what He does. And I know God can be trusted. And if I know anything it's this: followers of Jesus don't "just" do anything.

Just going to the store or just going to the coffee shop or just going to work or just sleeping around or just whatever is just a way to waste your life. And if there is something that should never be wasted it's your precious life. Jesus didn't just do anything. Jesus used His time as if it were on loan, as if it were important. Jesus was the master of stewardship. He was the great example in all things, even small things.

The ability to see everything as spiritual is a gift of God. But to take the trivial and throw it into the eternal is no easy task. It takes practice and discipline and hard work. We are not prone to it. We're prone to want to lay dead on the ocean floor. Seeing your life as a gift to use for the mission of God does not come naturally to us. We are masters of time wasting. We have a black belt in throwing away opportunities. We are quite competent at complaining instead of redeeming. We don't usually think about our time as something we will be held accountable for. We think of time as ours. But we must remember, nothing is ours.

I learned this lesson partially in New York City at six in the morning. I was on a mission trip and my job was to staple granola bars to fliers and stand at subway exits and ask people if they wanted free breakfast. It was freezing and I didn't have a warm jacket or gloves. I had a bad attitude and a small worldview. The fliers were for a local church in the area. They had only been having services for a few weeks. They were trying to serve their city in a simple, meaningful way, and in turn give out some invitations to their services. The fliers had three words printed largely on the front: "Are You Lonely?"

For six days my team and I stood at subway exits at six in the morning, asking people if they wanted free breakfast. We went home and if people asked what we did and how it went I said, "It was fine, we just passed out fliers." Really, what I wanted to say was, "It was freezing, and we did meaningless work."

A few months later I called our contact in New York and asked him how things were going. He said, "Josh, you wouldn't believe the response from those fliers. For the next few weeks after you guys left people came to our church holding crumpled fliers, saying thanks for the granola bar." I hung up the phone and shook my head. I told God I was sorry. I couldn't believe it—fliers, in New York City, at 6 A.M., stapled to granola bars, used by God.

If I've learned anything in the meantime it's that nothing is mine and nothing is meaningless. God can make anything come to life. Everything and everyone are redeemable.

## 32: the taste of art

Rich Mullins once played a new song for his bandmates and when he finished said, "All these songs are in me, it's just a question of whether or not I have the guts to pull them out." I think songs are in all of us but we don't have the guts to pull them out. I think Rich Mullins was right. So much of life takes guts.

A couple years ago I bought a concert DVD of Rich Mullins. It was filmed two months before his death. The part that moves me to this day is about halfway through, before he plays the song, "Sometimes by Step."

Rich is at the piano with his head down, just kind of sitting there. Eventually he starts playing gently, swaying back and forth in a trance, his fingers dancing over the keys, his bare feet bouncing up and down on the pedals.

He sits there and plays as if he's the only one in the room—as though God is the only one listening. Rich's long grey hair hung over his tired eyes, and his baggy sweater drooped off his tired body. He looked like he was thinking or praying or talking to himself.

After a while, Rich raises his head, looks at the crowd, takes a deep breath, and starts telling a story about prayer. He says the song he is about to play is a prayer song, and he says he likes to pray, though most times he finds it quite hard. He says the trouble with prayer is sometimes it turns into an attempt to impress God, not speak and listen to God. Rich Mullins says impressing God is impossible because God is already knocked out about us.

Then Rich says he likes to read Picasso, because when he looks at a Picasso painting it puts him into a coma. Rich said one time he read that Picasso wrote, "Good taste is the enemy of great art." Rich says taste is all about being cultured, polished, and refined but art is about being human.

He goes on to say that growing up he was a bit of a morose, depressed kid, and he stayed in his room a lot and wrote poetry to pass the time. He said people would tell him, "Cheer up Rich, God loves you." And he would respond, "Big deal, God loves everybody, that don't make me special, it just proves God ain't got no taste." Then Rich Mullins, quite reverently, almost as if he is remembering something says, "Thank God, that God has no taste and He willingly takes the junk of our lives and makes the greatest art in the world out of it."

Rich Mullins goes on to say, if the God of Scripture were as cultured and as civilized as most Christians wish He were, then He would be useless to Christianity. For if you want a religion or a God that makes sense, then Christianity is not the one, but if you want the religion and the God that makes life, then this is it.

Rich Mullins said the God of the Bible has no taste, has no concern to be entertained or impressed by the right words, spoken at the right moment, in just the right tone. He said in the Bible, if you really read it, you find all sorts of unrefined, uncultured, undignified people, and the most "un" of them all, the most completely Other, the wildest One in the whole Story, is God Almighty Himself.

Then Rich Mullins pauses, looks around, smiles and says, "I hope through the course of your life you encounter Him. But let me warn you, if you do, you'll need to hold on for dear life, or rather let go for dear life, maybe, is better."

## 33: the girl

Marriage is one of the greatest gifts of the meantime. There is something powerful and deeply God-honoring about a man and woman looking at each other, and before heaven and human, saying, "I do. Until Jesus returns or one of us goes to meet Him, I do." God knows God loves a covenant.

I met beautiful Amy in an airport in Nashville. I was wearing a zip-up hoodie and jeans. I was in a particularly good mood. Amy was wearing beauty. That's all I really remember.

When our eyes met at the baggage carousel everything went into slow motion and I swear I could hear music playing. It was the Nashville airport so I'm sure there was music playing.

I smiled—revealing a mouth full of braces—and said, "Hey."

She smiled, and said, "Hey."

Then, without much else to go on, I said, "Do I know you from somewhere? I really think I know you from somewhere."

She smiled again, "No, I don't think we've met."

"Well, I'm Josh, it's nice to meet you."

She put out her hand, "I'm Amy, it's nice to meet you too."

I may or may not have held her hand for an awkward amount of time. Who knows.

It turned out Amy and I were working the same summer camp and we were in Nashville for training. From the airport we split up and I didn't see her for a couple days. Eventually at training I saw her from across the room, and immediately, again, I heard music. I had to talk to her. So, I walked up, held out my hand, and said, "Hey, I'm Josh, do I know you from somewhere?"

She laughed, took my hand and said, "Josh, I don't know, are you sure we've met? I'm not from here."

Amy and I were married three years later on a summer day in California. Drew and Jason and Kurt, my brother Jeff and my best friend John were all there to cheer me on. I made them wear sweater vests, because on your wedding day you can do whatever you want—like make your best friends wear sweater vests.

June 7th was the most beautiful day in the history of Bakersfield. And the most beautiful day of my life. Something about weddings reminds me of the Kingdom. Because one day, we'll be at a wedding forever.

For a year and a half Amy and I dated long-distance. Our relationship unfolded and matured as I traveled with Drew and Jason. Amy and I spent hours and hours on the phone and we both have a hundred emails from the other saved in our inbox. We sent hand-written letters as well. At times it felt like I was off at war or something and my girl was back home staying in touch, keeping a shoebox full of letters under her bed.

I bought Amy coffee cups on my travels and shipped them to her. You could walk into our kitchen right now, open the cabinet above our coffee pot and see three shelves full of coffee cups, no two of which are the same. Our dating life took place everywhere. The first sight was an airport in Nashville, the first date was a show in Las Vegas, the first "I love you" was at a musical in Los Angeles, the first city we lived in was Pullman, Washington, and the proposal was on a beach in Santa Barbara.

The first fight, I don't remember.

My friend Max was the pastor at our wedding. He drove his family down from Cheyenne, Wyoming to perform the ceremony. I met Max a few years earlier when I was living in the car with the magician. He let us stay at his house and perform at his church. Max loved music and magic.

A few days before the wedding, Amy and I met Max at a coffee shop to talk about the ceremony. Max had been married to his wife Lynne for over 20 years. When he talked about her, or spoke of their wedding, you could see in his eyes how much he still loved her.

The night before my wedding I sat around a kitchen table with my best friends. The two decks of cards in front of us we never touched—too many stories to tell. The air was alive that night. I looked around the room and thought, "These are the men I want to play racquetball with when I'm Ronald Reagan's age."

Over the last year, Drew and Jason had been with me more than I'd been with myself, so their stories were the most current. But time didn't matter much, everyone's story felt like yesterday. My friend Phil was there, too. He'd been a faithful friend through college and the best guy in the world to have a cup of coffee with. He and his wife Lou later served in our church and over the years Lou became one of Amy's dearest friends.

A week before that night my best friend John got married. He and his wife flew in from their honeymoon to be in our wedding. John, Kurt, and I were college roommates. Kurt had been married to Jen for three years by then—we still couldn't believe she was with him.

When Kurt got back from his honeymoon he re-visited our apartment, knocked on the door, swung it open before we answered, and pronounced, "Last time I was in this apartment I was a child, but now, I re-enter as a man." Then he walked straight to the kitchen and started eating John's food.

All Kurt wanted to do around the kitchen table was make fun of John and ask him about honeymoon sex. John laughed a lot that night. He was sunburned and no longer a virgin. We all laughed a lot that night. I remember sitting there thinking relationships are a gift of God. Whether we are going through grief or joy, we were meant to go through it together.

The next day I got up early and spent time with Jesus. I told Him I was thankful for my friends and for Amy. I told Him I needed help. I told Jesus I couldn't be trusted to stay faithful on my own. I asked Jesus if He'd help me. I asked him if He would be near to us. He assured me He would. He told me He could be trusted and I shouldn't worry, and I shouldn't be afraid.

Then Jesus told me He thought the sweater vests were a great idea and I should tell Kurt to leave John alone. I agreed. Then Jesus told me He loved weddings and covenants, and He loved His Bride, the Church, and He loved Amy more than I ever could. I believed Him and knew He was right.

Our wedding made the world stand still. Amy walked down the aisle to Shane and Shane's version of "Before the Throne of God Above" and I could hardly breathe. Maybe it was the sweater vest or the heat or her beauty or the combination of the three, but when I heard, "Before the throne of God above, I have a strong and perfect plea, a great High Priest whose Name is Love, who ever lives and pleads for me," mixed with my girl—the girl—walking down the aisle, it overwhelmed me. I nearly crumbled.

The symbolism of the moment came at me from every angle. Amy was my bride—we are Jesus' Bride—this was our day—someday it will be Jesus' day. It all flooded my mind at once. It was the longest, most beautiful minute of my life.

The ceremony and reception were everything we dreamt they would be. We danced and ate and drank our fill. We were lovers in love lingering between two worlds. It was surely earth, but it surely felt and tasted like heaven. God was near to us. Jesus was present, like He had promised. The Spirit was in our hearts, on our lips and in our midst. The evening felt spiritual and natural—transcendent even. We celebrated, we remembered, we made a covenant, and God knows God loves when His people do that.

While Amy and I were signing our marriage certificate, Max said, "This was a special day. And you two made special vows." Then he leaned back in his chair and smiled, "Now if you ever want to break those vows, if you ever want a divorce, I think you should have to call everyone who was here back together and you should have to stand up and tell them you lied. You should have to give the gifts back, tell them you're sorry, you didn't mean it, you couldn't keep your word."

Then Max laughed, put his hands behind his head and said, "I think we wouldn't have as many divorces if couples had to do that."

## 34: the lessons

Amy taught me grace—terribly tangible grace. I thought I knew it before her. I didn't. I knew it in part, but the Holy Spirit is using her to teach me in whole.

When I confessed to Amy my past, she showed me grace. When I was quick to anger yesterday, she showed me grace. When I fail and lead poorly, she shows grace. When I buy things without asking, she shows me grace. When I don't do the dishes, she shows me grace. When I'm depressed and insecure and take it out on her, she shows grace. She is the grace of God in human form sharing a house with me. She is the light of the world ever shining into the darkness of my heart.

What I've learned about marriage is simple: it's not the great answer to our soul's great question. It's not Sunday. It's not what Amy and I were waiting on. We are waiting for Jesus, and we fell in love, so we made a covenant to wait together. Jesus is our hope. Jesus is the Greater Husband. He's our journey and destination. Marriage is daily choosing to walk to and with Jesus, together.

I told Amy early on I was no great rescue, to which she took my hand and lovingly said, "I know, and that's okay, because you're not the One I'm waiting on." For some reason I found that to be the most attractive thing she could say to me. To have a woman of God downgrade you in order to lift up Jesus is attractive. Just saying.

As fallen people, our hearts are full of questions and full of doubt, and many of the questions and doubt fall in the self-image and relationship realm. We want so badly to be accepted and pursued and loved and seen and known. We long for intimacy. We can't wait for someone to wait with. But if we're not careful we will esteem it too highly; it, though good, can become god, which is not good. It's beautiful and tragic. Wanting and exploring all those desires is beautiful in the right context, powerful in the right covenant, but, if out of place, tragic.

In my time of following Jesus, what I've seen pull people away from Him more than anything else has been poor choices in relationships.

The story goes something like this—a guy or a girl loves Jesus, has a sense of calling on his or her life. Then he or she gets into a relationship, starts making poor choices, then it's Saturday night and they're in a dark room with their shirt on the floor, and then Sunday morning at church they sit there wondering if God loves them, if their calling was even real—if God is even real.

We have to learn the opposite sex won't fulfill. We have to see the illusion and reject it wholesale. Amy and I were not broken on June 6th and whole on June 7th. We were made whole well before we were married. I was made whole when those 60-year-old missionaries in East Texas told me of the worth of Jesus. I've been whole since I was a teenager. I wasn't crying at the altar as Amy walked down the aisle because she was my missing link. I wept because Jesus graced me with someone to wait with. Jesus gave me the gift of a partner in the meantime. He gave me a safe context to have sex and be vulnerable and to grow in grace. Amy was given to me as a helper, as one to know and be known by. Our depth of intimacy is a shadow of a greater intimacy. Our nearness is to remind us of another nearness.

Marriage is about pruning sin out of our lives, not about providing happiness in our lives. Marriage is a fire and a garden. Amy purifies and prunes me. She tells me when I'm being selfish. She tells me when she's proud of me. She is my blind fan and loving critic. She is God's chosen agent of sanctification in my life. God wants me to be holy—to be like Jesus—and Amy is God's fire sent to burn the impurity out of me. She is my helper, my covenant, my best friend, my waiting mate—but not my rescue, never my Sunday.

The lesson we've learned is simple: Seek Jesus, and pray God brings someone along who will seek with you, wait well with you, and not laugh when they see you naked.

## 35: the track in Oregon

While Drew and I were traveling, doing music and magic, we dropped Jason off in the woods of North Carolina to do some music and magic of his own. He was going to serve two years with a wilderness camp ministry for boys who had two choices in life: go to a juvenile detention center or the woods of North Carolina.

Jason was perfect for the job. I don't know anyone who can climb trees or do handstands better than Jason. And even juvenile delinquents have to respect a guy who can climb trees and do handstands.

The leaders at the camp were called "chiefs." Drew and I started calling Jason, "Chief Jason," even before we dropped him off in the woods to help him grow accustomed. Chief Jason didn't mind much.

One afternoon we were traveling through Northern Oregon, along the Columbia River. The sun was setting over the hills, leaving the sky painted with colors no decent artist would put together, reminding us God was no decent artist. His taste is not like ours.

It had been a long day: Drew was driving, I was reading, Jason was sitting in the back seat silent—his only noise when he lifted his energy drink to his mouth. Jason was looking out the window mesmerized. In Northern Oregon there are tree farms along the side of the road. For miles and miles all you can see are rows of trees—hundreds of thousands of trees. It's beautiful and hypnotizing.

Eventually Jason spoke up, "Guys, I think something's wrong with me."

Drew and I replied, "What's wrong, Chief Jason?"

Jason took a long drink of energy, kept looking out the window, and said, "All guys my age think about are girls, all guys any age think about are girls, but all I can think about are those trees, and how right now I don't want a girl, I want Drew to pull over so I can climb every one of those trees."

After Jason was gone, Drew and I had no one to make us pull over and climb trees or use the bathroom. So we would say things like, "I mean, I don't have to use the bathroom, but if you pulled over and there was a restroom, I'd probably use it. I mean, probably, I don't have to go, but I would if I was standing in front of a toilet." Sometimes when we got bored and ran out of Smallville or Matt Chandler sermons we would set up the video camera and watch previous months of our travel footage.

Drew and Jason are highly competitive. Most days we drove to the rhythm of their back and forth banter. I sat in the front and read, Drew drove, and Jason sat in the back, sipping energy drinks, looking out the window, telling us all the amazing stuff he could do. He especially enjoyed telling us how fast he thought he could climb this or that.

Jason would say, "I bet I could climb to the top of that hill over there in 30 minutes."

Drew would say, "No way man, no way; that hill is too far, you'd never make it. You couldn't get from here to that fence in 30 minutes."

Jason would put down his energy drink, crawl into the front seat, put his face two inches from Drew's face and say in a slow aggressive tone, "Pull this truck over right now, and I'll be back in 30 minutes."

Drew would laugh, push Jason's face away, and keep driving.

Jason would go back into the back seat, look out the window again and start whispering to himself, "Oh yeah, 30 minutes, that's easy.

Drew, you better be glad you didn't pull this truck over. I'd show you. Oh yeah, easy."

Hills were not the only thing they talked about. Trees, mountains, rivers, energy drinks, everything was a bet. Everything was, "Oh yeah I could," and "No way, no way, not even close, you could never..." The most heated debate took place in Eugene, Oregon, on the University of Oregon campus. Jason and I ran cross-country together in college, so we had a mutual love for the long-distance legend and University of Oregon alumni, Steve Prefontaine.

As we drove around campus, debating which Steve Prefontaine movie was best, Jason, sipping a 64-ounce energy drink, said he bet he could run a lap around the University of Oregon track under 60 seconds. Drew started laughing and saying no way. Jason crawled into the front seat, put his nose in Drew's temple, and whisper-yelled, "Pull. This. Car. Over. Right. Now." This time, Drew did.

We walked onto the University of Oregon track and Jason started doing jumping jacks and pounding his chest. He had on soccer shoes, short black shorts, and a gray tee shirt. He didn't look like an Oregon track athlete, but we figured he could fake it for one lap. Jason started stretching, looking at the track, and talking to himself. "Oh yeah, 60 seconds, this is easy. No problem. Drew is going down this time. Oh yeah, he's going down."

When Jason was done with the toe touches and pep talk, he walked to the starting line. Drew and I sat in the bleachers, our stopwatches ready. Jason took a few deep breaths, shook his legs a bit, lifted his head, let out a war cry, and started running.

He was faster than we expected. He rounded the first curve way ahead of pace. Drew and I knew we were in trouble. Our only hope now was that fatigue would set in, or a maintenance man would tackle him. Drew said, "Just wait until 250 meters, he'll catch a cramp and come jogging in the last 150 with a smile and excuse."

Jason rounded the second curve and didn't slow down. He was running like a man possessed. The fatigue never set in and down the last straight away the maintenance men thought he was on the track team. Jason finished the lap in 57 seconds. As he crossed the finish line we were cheering him on, happy to have lost.

I held up my watch and yelled, "57 seconds!"

Jason lost his mind. He started jumping around shouting, "Oh yeah, oh yeah, I knew it, I told you, I knew it! Drew, you should have never pulled over!"

As Jason came off the track we hugged and congratulated him. Then, as if a switch were flipped, his gloating turned to burping, "I'm going to be sick." Jason ran behind the bleachers and threw up 64-ounces of energy drink. After filming him throw up for five minutes we walked out of the stadium feeling like we had all won. Jason ran a lap under 60 seconds and Drew and I had our friend on film throwing up under the bleachers at the University of Oregon.

As we got in the truck and started driving, Jason laid in the back seat trying to get control of his body. After a few minutes he mumbled,

"Josh, I could feel him as I ran."

"Who could you feel?" I asked, "Jesus?"

"No. Not Jesus." Jason said, "Steve Prefontaine."

## 36: the church plant

Eventually, the road wore us out. Drew and I wanted real friends and a real bed. We grew weary of telling the same jokes and same stories. We were bored with being cool for five hours.

When you go into a city for a weekend and spend most of your time on stage everyone thinks you invented the wheel. Everyone smiles at you and pays for your food. But it only lasts about five hours. Then you get lonely, find yourself daydreaming at the dinner table. You want community. You need it. It's natural—necessary. Your lungs long for real air, not hot air.

Toward the end of that year, Drew and I spent most of our drive-time talking about who we wanted to be and what kind of life we wanted to have when we were Ronald Reagan's age. We decided if we made it to Ronald Reagan's age, we wanted to be sitting around on someone's porch drinking coffee and telling stories. We wanted to grow old and awesome, and dress however we felt like dressing, and smile when we talked to younger people. We wanted a hint of wisdom in our eyes. We wanted to be the kind of people who could be trusted, the kind of old men who could tell a great story. We wanted long lists of great stories. We wanted to be friends who grew old together and played racquetball together and started movements together. We wanted to be the church.

One stretch of the music and magic tour took us to the Pacific Northwest. Specifically Pullman, Washington. We performed at Washington State University for an evening and afterward went to Denny's for a late-night breakfast. The irony is, Drew's and my story started over a late-night breakfast.

It was our senior year of college and we were studying for a Christian Doctrine final. At two in the morning, two days before our graduation from East Texas Baptist University, I asked Drew, "What are you doing with your life?" That question led to the music and magic and a year of road life. Who knew that conversation would also lead us a year later to another breakfast place two thousand miles away from East Texas, again at two in the morning, with the same question on the table, "What are you doing with your life?"

Drew said he wasn't sure. Then he asked me the same question. I looked at my cup of coffee, then looked up and said, "I think I want to start a church here in Pullman."

A week later we were at the Pullman Denny's again, this time at a reasonable hour, and this time with a team of local pastors talking about what it might look like if we started a church. Eight months later, Drew and I moved from our homes in Texas to make a new home in Washington. We drove separate cars and talked on walkie-talkies until Wyoming. When our batteries ran out, we drove in silence for hours, speeding up to pass each other and wave every once in a while. Then Drew called me and said the trailer tire was smoking. We were in Montana and it was well below freezing. Our tire was flat and it was getting dark. We pulled over and I ran back and got in Drew's car. We sat on the side of the road in Montana laughing and talking about how cold it was.

We called Jason and told him how hard we had it. He told us he lived in the woods and killed snakes with his bare hands so we should be man enough to change a tire in Montana. We hung up and made a plan: we would turn up the heater in Drew's car and take five-minute shifts changing the tire. We only had one jacket so we would share. It was miserable and the tire was jammed into the trailer's wheel cover so we had to bang the metal away with our lug wrench. It took about an hour, but we fixed it. We called Jason and told him we did it. He wasn't impressed. He said yesterday he ate a spider.

For the first time in a year, we decided not to sleep in our cars. We thought we had earned a hotel stay, so we paid to sleep at the Hampton Inn. The next morning we slept late and stayed until the maid made us leave or pay for another night. It was glorious. We called Chief Jason and told him about the maid. This time he laughed.

Pullman became my Africa—where I brought my life, not my camera. Drew and I joined a team of dreamers and started a church. Ten months after our arrival in the Northwest we had our first public worship service. That was four years ago.

## 37: the beautiful mess

Church planting is exhilarating and exhausting. Just thinking about it makes me want to take a nap. I woke up the morning of our church launch feeling like I was getting married or something. It was before I was married so I didn't know what being married felt like, but I was sure it would feel something like this. My legs were light—my heart was racing. I felt alive, like a kid on Christmas. Drew felt the same way. There is emotion and exhilaration in the air the day your church launches.

Our team was having breakfast at a friend's house so Drew and I drove over talking about how crazy it was that we were on a team of people who started a church. That evening at 5p.m. the seven original dreamers: Drew, Megan, Keith, Paige, Kim, Amy and myself, held hands in a circle, bowed our heads, closed our eyes, exhaled together, and prayed a prayer of thanksgiving to the God of the Church, who makes impossible things possible, invisible things visible, and broken people whole. We asked Him to be near, and He was. At 5:30 P.M. the doors opened. We started a church.

---

Sin, I've always known. Grace, I had to be taught. Christ taught me first and He teaches me still. He extends grace after grace into the depths of my secrets. His diligence towards me—His steadfast pursuit— has protected me from me for years. He has taken the mess of my life and made something beautiful out of it.

I don't know about other people, but every one of my sins is the same. No matter what it's called, if you spend enough time examining it, you find beneath it, hidden away in the darkest of dark cellars, *pride* is providing the blood flow to sin's heartbeat. Pride is lust for God's job. It's the source of darkness. It's anti-God and pro-self. It was the birth-right passed down to me even before I was born. Pride is the human experience. It makes sin easy and grace difficult. Pride makes confession and repentance torture.

Being taught grace is similar to being taught confession and repentance. For if we never confess and repent of our sins, there is no opportunity for grace to kick down the dark cellar door of our prideful heart. Repentance is coming clean; it's prying the cellar door open. Repentance is raw, no excuses, no secrets. Repentance lets light in.

But, it's messy and in community it can be awkward. In the presence of repentance, people who aren't good at grace will want to turn their eyes away. But to those who don't shift their eyes, the mess can become beautiful.

When we first started our church I had a drummer named Mike who played in the band. Mike had a rough past but was faithful to our rehearsals and was working to be faithful to Jesus. Mike and I probably had coffee twenty times. He was funny and likeable, but behind his eyes you could see grave clothes.

Mike attended my small group but rarely spoke. In that setting, he was quiet and reserved, like he was afraid of someone noticing his baggage. Maybe he didn't feel like he fit in, or maybe he felt like his struggles were still too strong and everyone else in the room had it all together. I should have told Mike the perfect Christians were pretending. I should have told Mike I had grave clothes too. It might have helped him feel normal.

One Sunday Mike was late to set-up. Our church, at the time, started at 6p.m. and we set up at 3:00 P.M. At around 3:30 I called Mike. It went straight to voicemail. At 4:30 everyone was calling Mike. He'd never been late before and we were getting worried. Around 5:00 P.M., Keith, our pastor, got a call from the hospital saying Mike was there. He'd overdosed on alcohol the night before and had a blood alcohol level capable of shutting down your kidneys. They had him on medications and an I.V.

Three days later at our small group meeting, Mike came in and I hugged him—told him I was glad he was okay and it was good to see him. When our group conversation started, I asked a basic icebreaker question, which was typical. Then, out of nowhere, Mike stands up. There are probably 30 people in the living room, scattered all throughout couches and chairs and carpet, in a poor attempt at a circle. No one ever stood up.

Mike stood up, took his hat off and said, "Hello everyone, my name is Mike. Some of you know me, and for those who don't, my name is Mike and I play drums in the worship band."

He was looking down and rubbing the brim of his hat with one hand. Mike looked up and said, "I know we are supposed to talk about the sermon from Sunday, but I wanted to confess something to everyone first if that's okay."

"Of course, Mike," I said.

The room went silent. Then Mike said, "As some of you may have noticed, there were no drums on Sunday. I was supposed to play, but I was in the hospital, because on Saturday night I drank so much alcohol my friends had to take me to the ER to get my stomach pumped. I passed out Saturday night and didn't wake up until Sunday afternoon." Then Mike started to cry. He gripped his hat, pulled it to his chest and said, "I'm so sorry, everyone. I can't believe what I did. I'm so sorry."

Mike sat down quickly and put his face in his hands and wept. In a silent room filled with 30 peers, Mike sat there and wept. I walked over and knelt down next to him and said, "I'm proud of you, Mike, I know that wasn't easy."

Then I invited everyone to pray, and for the next 20 minutes that's what we did. And throughout the room you could hear others start to cry—probably because brokenness is contagious. Eventually, everyone in the living room prayed for Mike. Everyone invited the God of grace to invade his darkness.

When we finished praying Mike gave many of us a hug. Then we went on and had the best discussion we had all year.

There's something powerful about brokenness—something healing about honesty. Mike openly repented, was fully exposed and vulnerable and he was accepted all the same. There's power in being known and loved anyway. There's release when you close your eyes and share your guts then open your eyes and realize no one ran away.

I think more often than not, people don't run away from sinners, but sinners run away from people. I think this is why we usually only speak of our sin in the past tense—especially big sin. We distance ourselves from the graphic nature of it. We don't call it dirty. We say we used to struggle, but now—praise God—we've gained victory. This has always made me nervous, because distance and vagueness never bring healing. Healing comes when you're broken publicly and grace is offered openly. God will forgive you, but He won't heal you; He has chosen to let the Church do that.

One of my favorite singer/songwriters, Derek Webb, says the best thing that could ever happen to you is that your sin be broadcast on the 5 o'clock news. That way when you see your neighbors the next day, and they ask about what they heard on the news, you can say, "It's true—all of it—and that's why I need a Savior." Small sin needs a small Savior and big sin needs a big Savior and we all have big sin needing big healing.

I think Mike hated what he did. I think he felt shame and frustration first, but then I think somewhere in the process Mike's shame turned to hatred. I think that's why he could stand up and say what he said. He wasn't speaking as a man just saying "Sorry," he was speaking as a man saying, "I need help, from Jesus and from you." This is the trouble with pride. Prideful people can't hate sin. They are too busy hiding it, rationalizing it, pretending time will heal it and distance will comfort. Prideful people hate that they may be found out, they rarely hate that they've committed treason. They don't even see it that way. Everything is not that bad. Everything is fine. Or, in prideful apathy, everything is "just the way it is," and nothing can really be done about it.

Mike hated the way it was. He hated that he knew sin so well. And he knew the only weapon against pride is exposure. The only weapon against darkness is light. So, at the first chance he had, he stood up, took his hat off and repented. Mike didn't care about his reputation anymore. He cared about reconciliation.

## 38: the nametag

Dr. Bob used to say, "God will allow you 5 years of bad sermons if you preach 30 years of good ones." With our church approaching 5 years old I wonder if that translates to all areas of ministry. I've heard growing up as a pastor's kid is hard. I don't know—my dad works in the oil fields. But I know first-hand growing up as a pastor is hard. It takes a while to get used to the title, the truth, and the turmoil. It takes a while to swallow the term.

But, there comes a point when you look in the mirror and say, "I'm a pastor, my church looks at me as one of its pastors, I need to walk in the calling of pastor, it's what God's invited me into, so I need to start being it."

There's something I've always appreciated about Saul turned Paul in the Bible. When Jesus turns him to Paul, he just starts calling himself an Apostle. Paul starts all of his letters using this title, making sure people know who's writing. Trouble is, an Apostle—by definition—was one who had been with Jesus.

The 12 disciples who had been with Jesus were called Apostles— but they were the only ones. No one else used that title. It was a closed title, given to a closed group, by Jesus himself. But, Paul used the title for his calling. It's as if when Paul called himself an Apostle, he's saying,

"You know the 12, how they're Apostles, yeah, well, me too."

Paul never spent time with Jesus like the 12. He never slept on the ground next to Him or sat around a campfire with Him. He didn't know Jesus' laugh or the lines in His face. He'd never physically touched Him, ate with Him or prayed with Him. But, Paul had his own encounter, and with that encounter came a title.

Paul—over a period of time no doubt—begins to identify with the Apostles as "one who had been with Jesus." Paul didn't ask for permission. He didn't have to. Jesus gave him permission. Jesus ordained Paul. And Jesus ordains us. It's different, our story, and Paul's. But it's similar. Without Jesus coming and knocking us off our horse we would still be riding the wrong direction, forever lost. But Jesus came to us, just like He did to Saul, and said, "No more."

I wonder if Paul struggled the first time he wrote the words, "Paul, an apostle, appointed not by man, but by Christ Jesus the Lord." I wonder if he questioned his worth or ran his hands through his hair and looked up at the ceiling wondering if he was saying the right thing. I wonder if it took him a couple years to get comfortable with the title.

No doubt God appointed him, but no doubt, he doubted. The Apostles had three years and an eye-witnessed resurrection to affirm their calling; Paul had an isolated event—a life-changing event, but a single event nonetheless.

It was years before God used Paul to write his first letter to a church, and by that time he might have been more comfortable in his shirt, but before that, I wonder how he dealt with the meantime. I wonder how he learned his new name in the waiting.

---

Telling someone you are going to start a church is not hard. It sounds ambiguous and interesting and usually people don't know how to place it. They say, "Interesting," and take a sip of their drink while turning to peer at the door, wondering how long this explanation is going to take. Telling someone you're a pastor was difficult for me—at least at first. It's like I wanted someone to stand next to me and say, "It's okay, you can say that. You are a pastor. Relax. Just breathe."

I wasn't afraid. I didn't want to use another term. I mean, I've never told someone I was a spiritual-coach or life-mentor or cultural-architect or something. To me, those terms are more exhausting. It's just when I first told people I was a pastor I waited for the door to bust open and someone to come in with a badge that said Apostle and cut me off. I kept thinking I'd hear laughing. It doesn't matter what your business card says, if you're not wearing your title humbly, as a nametag Jesus wrote and stuck to your chest Himself, then you're not what you say you are.

Part of the problem for me was my age. Drew and I were 24 when we started saying we were pastors. We weren't married, didn't have kids or a house. We owned a few books and a bike. We ate cereal two meals a day. It's hard to say you're a pastor when you eat cereal two meals a day. I don't know why, but it seems there should be a rule—real pastors don't eat much cereal. We were learning, growing, gaining experience one fall at a time.

Keith, at least, was 29. He'd been married for a while, had a son already and a baby girl on the way. He owned a house and a lawnmower, and from what I could tell, didn't eat much cereal—more of an oatmeal guy. Drew and I started trying to get married and eat better. We went and priced lawnmowers. We started going to bed early and we quit watching midnight reruns of American Gladiators. It was a start.

What we lacked in experience we made up for in passion. We told everyone we knew—and anyone who would listen—about our future church. After we unloaded our trailer into our first home in Pullman, we went to eat at Denny's. Our waitress' name was Jessica. She took our order and asked where we were from—probably because Drew still talked like he had a piece of straw in his mouth. I tried to kill my accent in

Montana, but it was still breathing. Barely, but breathing. Drew's though, was thriving, showing off even.

We told Jessica we had lived in Pullman for four hours. We told her we were going to start a new church and she should come. "So, you guys are pastors?" she asked. Drew and I looked at each other for what felt like a year. I started scratching my neck. One of us almost said spiritual-architect or life-coach, but instead I said simply, "Yeah, something like that." She said, "Cool," and walked away. I took my jacket off because I was sweating.

Four hours in, two 24-year-olds at Denny's were willing to say they were starting a church, but weren't willing to say they were pastors. Four hours in, I realized this is going to be grown up work. This new identity was going to take some getting used to and at some point, I was going to have to come to terms with Jesus calling me a pastor.

I picture it going something like this: Jesus takes a Sharpie and starts writing something on a nametag.

Midway through, I realize what He's doing.

I say nervously, "Jesus, are you sure?"

P-A-S-T

"Jesus, I mean let's talk about this,"

P-A-S-T-O

"Jesus, the girl at Denny's, Jessica, You know her, right? Well anyway, she asked if I was a pastor and I bailed out of the conversation, are You sure You want to call me a..."

PASTOR.

As Jesus puts the cap on the sharpie and peels the nametag from its sheet, He looks at me and says, "I'm sure." And as He touches my chest to make the nametag stick, I feel something. Maybe it's what Paul felt the first time he wrote Apostle. It's a weight. A weight that never felt so heavy and so light.

Jesus touches my chest and suddenly I like the nametag. It's simple, one word, six letters, but it fits. And I want it to fit. Because Jesus wrote it, and He put the name on me, and when Jesus puts a name on you, you're honored to wear it. As Jesus leans back to take a look, I press my whole hand against the tag, not to cover the name, but to make sure it sticks.

---

If I'm honest I'd tell you, when Jesus offered me the nametag I wasn't sure I should wear it. I didn't think I was worthy. I figured there was a book somewhere that said those who had sex before marriage, or ever drank beer, or who had family issues, under no circumstance, could be a pastor. And even if that book didn't exist, I wasn't confident I could endure as a pastor. Sometimes I thought, give me a week and someone will find this nametag in the trash by my desk.

Or, my biggest fear was, somehow I'd deceived myself to believe Jesus offered me the nametag, when in the end, He didn't really offer it to me. In some delusional moment I scribbled my own name down and when Jesus came back in the room, He said, "What are you doing? Give me that nametag."

---

Wearing pastor is wearing weary—at least at first. It's a life on display, leading and serving others, while dueling your selfish nature to the death. That's why it's so important to have Jesus' handwriting on your nametag.

Walking into church work without the calling of Jesus is dangerous. Not because church work is all bad, or intended to break the weak, but because it's eternal. It's doing work where heaven and hell and earth collide and inviting others to follow you there. It's standing on behalf of people on earth, knowing one day, you will stand on behalf of these people in heaven.

Jesus will lovingly judge pastors more harshly, so you want Him to have appointed you to said judgment. You want to daily look down and make sure He wrote your name on the tag, not you.

I'm learning as a pastor to tread lightly, for I'm walking on holy ground. The good news is, this holy ground is not new ground. It's covered in the blood and footprints of previous men and women who laid down their Saturday in assurance of gaining Sunday.

The ground I stand on in Pullman is really not the ground at all. It's the shoulders of previous saints who toiled the ground in order that we might plant and reap. Sometimes, when days are long and people are difficult, I think about that. I think about previous pastors in previous generations playing their part—inviting me to play mine.

Sometimes, I think about those missionaries at R.A. camp, and I'm encouraged and reminded how worthy God is. I hope one day Amy and I can put our old wrinkled hands together in front of a group of young people and tell them stories of God's faithfulness.

The wise will kneel down and touch the old tracks, they will put their ear to the ground hoping to learn from the ones who've gone before—hoping to make some sense of the winding road and the snare at every turn.

When you're young, though, you're reckless, and you don't know what to look for. And, truth is, you're not interested in looking to anyone or listening to anyone. You don't realize many wiser people have walked before you—you think you're the only wise one; you don't need someone else to lead the way.

I was this way. I walked into church planting with a heart full of submission issues. I didn't care what was on the ground, I wanted to shed my own blood, leave my own prints. Every rookie wants this. But every veteran will tell you, fear not rookie, you're going to bleed, whether I help you or not—blood's coming—but at least follow me, and I'll keep you from losing a limb, or worse, your soul.

## 39: the adoption

The beauty of Christianity is there is no way to tell who's who. If you were to line up everyone in the world who follows Christ, you wouldn't be able to tell who's who or what's what. Everyone is different. Followers of Christ come in all backgrounds and sizes. From every tribe and tongue are people who call on the name of Jesus.

The similarity is internal. The mark is simple: we've gone from being an orphan to being adopted. Every Christian should have an understanding in their soul that who they are is not their own. They're bought. There was a price on our life we couldn't afford. And it was paid on our behalf. Our skin color didn't affect this purchase. Our pocketbook wasn't taken into consideration before the transaction was made. We are bought, and the bought ones are similar, simply in the truth of their purchase.

The primary picture in the Bible for salvation is adoption. I understand adoption because when I was 15, a man who was not my biological father, went to court on my behalf and told a judge, "This one's mine," and pointed to me.

I remember standing there proud to have a dad. I remember feeling wanted. I left the room with a legal name change. I walked out no longer who I used to be—my name, my identity, my bloodline, changed.

A couple months ago my friend Ed came to Washington State to talk about adoption at our University. Ed's a preacher, and the most natural evangelist I've ever met. Ed can bring up Jesus anywhere, to anyone, and it feels normal.

His job in Pullman was to educate and inspire students about the need for international adoption. Ed did so much more than that. For me, as I listened to Ed tell his story about adopting his son from Ethiopia, I learned about another Father, who also adopted; who's always adopting.

Ed said adoption is costly. He and his wife Stephanie had to liquidate most of their assets to be able to pay the price. They flew to Ethiopia twice and on more than one occasion weren't sure the process was going to go through.

Ed said the whole journey was emotionally and physically exhausting. Until that is, they held their son.

On the final day of the trip to Ethiopia, Ed and Stephanie and their three daughters were in the orphanage preparing to leave with their son. As they walked to the door holding their baby boy the lady working the front desk asked for the clothes their son was wearing. She said the orphanage needed to wash the clothes and give them to another child in need. Ed and Stephanie took the clothes off their son and handed them to the worker.

Then they stood there for a minute, two steps from the door of the orphanage, holding their naked son. As Ed told the story, I remember him starting to speak slower—more deliberately—almost as if he wanted students to hear the story behind the story. Adoption was the point Ed was there to press home—we were putting on an event hoping to bring awareness and funding to the education of six young men in Ethiopia. Ed was not there to tell the crowd about Jesus. But Ed, being Ed, was trying to tell them without telling them.

We put on two events back-to-back that night. Between the first and second presentation Ed came up to me and gave me a hug. I told him he did great. He told me, "Josh, without the Gospel, this whole presentation is lacking."

When Ed got to the point in the story where he and his wife were at the door holding their son, he slowed down and said, "There I was, in the middle of Africa, holding a naked baby boy, knowing one step inside the door he was just another child in need of parents, and one step outside the door he would have my inheritance." Ed walked out the door with his son and Stephanie took off her backpack. Inside she had new clothes for baby Lawson.

On the steps of the orphanage they put new clothes on their son. They gave him covering; they give him a new name. Ed said, "I looked at 2-year-old Lawson and told him, 'I'm your father, this is your mother, these are your sisters. Don't be afraid, we'll take care of you, everything we have is yours.'"

Adoption saves. There are no better words to describe it. Salvation adopts and adoption saves. It creates a secure bond working itself out through a bad situation gone well. God the Father looked down on Ed and as they walked over the threshold of the orphanage with Lawson, God whispered to Ed, "What I did for you, Ed, it's like this."

## 40: the despair

Recently I read a quote by Hans Kung. A lot of smart people I know say Hans Kung is one of the most brilliant theologians of our time. During an interview, Dr. Kung was asked about his faith, or more pointedly how his belief system has worked out over the years. He responded, "It's been a long time since I've believed, truthfully I no longer believe at all. I know."

Hans Kung made me wonder if we're obsessed with belief, wandering from such to such, cause to cause, knowing little of what we believe and why. I wonder if Hans quit believing because at some point belief wasn't good enough. In order to carry on, he needed to know. I wonder if after years of serving people, not causes, Hans began to know what Jesus meant when He spoke of taking care of the least, not simply believing it might be a good idea.

Change will come and hope will rise when we realize the world around us is not full of good causes, but full of Jesus requesting a cup of water, a moment of consideration, a pack of cigarettes, a bowl of soup, a visit in prison.

Here is why I think what Hans Kung said is so important: Beliefs may usher us into the deepest needs of the world, but be assured—upon arriving there—we will need more than belief to carry on. In that place full of the world's deepest needs, we may not find comfort, we may not easily access hope, a way out, or a way of change, and it will be there—in the toughest moments—where belief is not sufficient.

In that place—among that darkness and need—we must cling to something deeper than belief—something we know, Someone we know—because knowledge of Someone is a stubborn thing and not easily pushed aside or swayed. I look forward to the day when belief is not enough. I look forward to knowing what Hans does.

---

Despair is a word I can't remember my mother using until after her time in jail. I can understand why. Despair is a delicate word. It's vulnerable and brutal. To tell someone you're in despair is to whisper a soul cry.

Paul tells the Corinthians, we are troubled on every side, yet not distressed; we are perplexed, but not in despair; persecuted, but not forsaken; struck down, but not destroyed. He's writing hope to a people who feel forsaken and destroyed and are wandering toward despair.

Writing, speaking, living, breathing hope is the remedy of despair—if even there is such a thing. The planting of hope is the work of God. And in this sense, we are the workers of God. And planting, speaking, living, breathing hope is the task. But the despair is rooted in a depth we rarely delve. The despair, when set in, is set in the inner being of who we are; it's there for one reason—to rival our foundation, that is, the love of God.

The great spiritual writer and theologian Henri Nouwen went through six months of anguish and despair during his years as a priest and professor. He kept a journal through the process that was later published as *The Inner Voice of Love*. The book is filled with promptings and promises Nouwen wrote to himself. He called them spiritual imperatives, or what was later known as 63 self-commands. The writings are raw and wrought with darkness and light. Nouwen experienced what he described as, "One long scream coming from a place I didn't know existed, a place full of demons."

In one of his imperatives, "Always Come Back To The Solid Place," he writes these words: "You must believe in the yes that comes back when you ask, 'Do you love me?' You must choose this yes even when you do not experience it." And he goes on to say, "Right now you feel nothing except emptiness and the lack of strength to choose. But keep saying, 'God loves me, and God's love is enough.' You have to choose the solid place over and over again and return to it after every failure."

Henri Nowen believed in and knew the love of God. He had—as maybe you and I have—an intellectual understanding regarding God's love, but until we feel the love of God in our bones, we have not yet known it. Until we apply the love of God into the deepest places of our despair, we have not yet found home base. We are still wandering.

I've felt moments of emptiness, twinges of torment, but nothing to the degree of what Nowen experienced. But between the most difficult and simple degrees, the similarities are haunting. The question we find looming about in the despair is both the most complicated and simple question in all the world, "God, do you love me?"

## 41: the presence

My grandpa died recently. He battled a bad heart for years. Towards the end, he had to carry an oxygen bottle with him everywhere. He and my brother and I went fishing two months before he died and he had tubes in his nose to help him breathe.

It was hard to see him so frail, because he wasn't frail. Not to me anyway. My grandpa was the toughest man I knew. But life and heart disease had worn him down. His Sunday was coming, you could see it in his eyes, hear it in his voice. He was so tired, so ready to be with Jesus— in a city with no hospitals or pills.

My mom called me on the morning of Good Friday and asked me to pray for Grandpa because he wasn't breathing well and the doctors wanted to life-flight him to San Antonio. She called back 20 minutes later saying he didn't make it. We sat on the phone silent and miserable. Living far away from family burns in these moments.

I wrote about Grandpa's death on the Internet, processing my thoughts, and asking people to pray for my family. The picture and blog I posted got over 250 notifications. But, I only got one phone call. Only one person, my friend Phil, picked up the phone and called me and prayed for me. Even some of my closest friends locally didn't know how to serve me. They liked my post online but never told me in person they were sorry.

Now, many others did. Many of my church friends loved me and served me and asked questions and hugged me. My church staff even pooled money together and sent my grandmother flowers. They were gracious, and the flowers were a beautiful blessing to my grandmother. She put them front and center on her windowsill.

I have a friend named Bart. Bart's mother died many years ago. While having dinner with Bart, he told me he could still name the last three people in the room with him when he got the news his mother died. He told me a few weeks ago one of his best friends lost her mom. Bart said he drove four hours to her house with one goal: be the last one in the room. Bart sat there with her, not saying a word, just being present, just sitting there; after everyone else left, he kept sitting there. Knowing, years from now, she'd never forget this, and knowing—because he'd experienced it—the power of presence, the depth of sitting in silence together.

I almost didn't go to my grandfather's funeral. Plane tickets were expensive and it was Easter weekend. He passed away on Good Friday and the funeral was Tuesday morning. Eventually, Amy and Drew pushed me to buy a ticket so I made the trip. My grandfather meant a lot to me. We were close. He wasn't a distant relative I barely knew. He and I had spent years and years together. And your oldest grandson should be at your funeral.

When I arrived in Texas, Monday at 2:00 A.M., the money didn't matter. My uncle and I embraced and cried. My mother got out of bed and comforted me. The family woke up the next morning at 6:00 A.M., brewed coffee and sat in the dining room trying to speak. We couldn't. But we were present. And being present was enough.

I could have called. I could have video-chatted. I could have just sent some money to help with funeral costs. But none of those would have been the same as sitting in the dining room at 6:00 A.M. the morning of the funeral with my family. Nothing would have had the same effect. The power was in the presence.

---

It reminded me of a sermon I heard by a guy named David Platt. David Platt was talking about going from your neighborhood to the nations. He said a lot of people think they don't have to go on mission trips; they can just send money to support the mission. David Platt said he wrestled with that for a while. Would it benefit the people in Sudan more for me to send $4,000 or for me to send myself for a month for $4,000, he asked?

While David Platt was in Sudan he was talking to a local pastor. The pastor had come to a training David led. David Platt said they were sitting in the shade under the scorching African sun, in the middle of war-torn Sudan, drinking hot tea and the local pastor said, almost out of nowhere, "David, do you know what a true brother is?" David Platt said, "No. Tell me what a true brother is."

The local pastor took a sip of hot tea and looked at David Platt and said, "David, we have a lot of people send money. A lot of good organizations have tried to help us in our trouble. But, David, a true brother is not just someone who sends money. A true brother is someone who comes and sits with you in your greatest time of need. David, you are a true brother."

David Platt says you can't just send money. You have to send yourself. David Platt went on to say, "Aren't you glad God didn't just send money, aren't you glad God didn't just pray for us, aren't you glad God was willing to send His only Son Jesus, and aren't you glad Jesus took on flesh and dwelt among us?"

---

During one of those nights in Texas, I stayed up late drinking coffee and talking to my grandmother. We talked about Grandpa, and laughed and cried, and made our way into a conversation about life and death and God. I asked her questions about Catholicism and she asked me about our church. She explained to me why she prays to Mary. First she clarified, she doesn't pray "to" Mary, she "asks Mary to pray for her."

My grandmother told me she is not good enough to ask Jesus for something. She said, "Josh, who am I to ask Jesus for something. I'm just a sinner. I'd rather ask Jesus' mom to pray for me. If she prays for me Jesus will listen. If I pray Jesus might listen, but if Mary does, there's a better chance of being heard."

My grandmother told me she loves the parables. I asked her if she knew the parable of the Prodigal Son. She told me it was one of her favorites. I asked her if she'd ever thought about God being a Father who runs to us when we return home from a season of sin. She said no. My grandmother had never put God in the story. She never put herself in the story either. To her it was just a parable; no one had ever explained it.

As I talked to my grandmother that night I was overwhelmed by how much I loved her. I was so thankful God gave me grandparents. It had only been a day and I already missed my grandpa so much, but talking to Grandma about Jesus was helping me heal.

My grandma asked me to explain the parable to her. She asked who God was and who we were in the story. She said, "Joshua, tell me what Jesus meant."

When I told her the Father was God and we were the Prodigal coming home I watched her demeanor change. She wasn't sure it was legal. For God to run seemed impossible, because of course, God is so serious.

I told my grandmother she was a daughter of God and so was Mary. I said, "Grandma, when you pray, God hears you, just as well as He would have heard Mary when she was on Earth." When I told my grandma she and Mary were both equally adopted daughters of God she shifted in her chair.

She said, "Joshua, I'm a sinner."

"So was Mary, Grandma." I said. "Jesus died and rose for the sinners. No one is good, Grandma. Not even Mary. Only Jesus."

Grandmother looked at her coffee, moving her fingers over the lip of the cup. Time stood still as she thought about—for the first time—how God the Father viewed her.

In the midst of her thinking, I took her hand and said, "Grandma, God loves you, He's pleased with you. You and Mary are sisters in Christ."

She shook her head, unwilling to hear me at first. Her hand stayed in mine and I said, "Grandma, you don't need Mary to go between you and Jesus, you need Jesus to go between you and God, and He's already done that. Because of Jesus, you can go as confidently to God as Mary can."

Eventually my grandmother asked me if I was telling the truth.

She looked at me, half smiled and said, "I don't know, Joshua, are you sure?"

"I'm sure," I said.

She laughed, "How sure are you?"

"I'm really sure, Grandma. Really, really sure."

## 42: the person and place of heaven

I don't know much about God and neither do you. It's not that God is unknowable; it's just there's too much to know. In light of the potential knowledge of things to know about God, we don't know much. And I don't think it's just us, I think the person in the world who knows the most about God still doesn't know much about God. However, though we don't know much, we know enough. Sufficient knowledge is surely available.

God has lived forever. Before I knew God, the thought of forever scared me. I would lie in bed at night and think of death as a deep sea of darkness, the never-ending end. I thought about people lying in their graves and felt hopeless. They will never rise again I'd say, and someday that will be me. It's torture to think like that.

Something unique about our time in history is God lives in us. For as long as God has been, and for as long as the world's been, I count it quite the privilege to be of the generations in which God dwelled not simply among, but in.

In the Old Testament certain people had the Spirit of God on them, or even in them, but their relationship with God was not the same as ours. The Old Covenant was based on grace through faith and adherence to the Law, not grace through faith and evidence of the Holy Spirit.

The New Covenant speaks of God leaving a deposit of the Holy Spirit in us, evidence not only external, but internal. The Holy Spirit comforts, counsels, and reminds us daily that God will return for us. The Holy Spirit is God's yes to the question Henri Nowen posed, "God, do you love me?"

Jesus spoke of God as if He were available, and of heaven as if it were a person and place that could be touched. Jesus told parables not only defining the place of heaven, but the Person of heaven. The story of the Great Banquet, for instance—in which the rich people ignore the invitation and the Master of the house sends word to the poor and the broken to come in and eat and drink—does not only speak of the party, but just as much speaks of the Master. The party is about the Master; the invitation is not only to a place, but also to a Person.

I remember hearing a sermon one time by a guy named Paris Reidhead called "Ten Shekels and a Shirt." At the end of the sermon Paris Reidhead says, "I'm going to say to you dear friend, if you're out there without Christ, you come to Jesus Christ and serve Him as long as you live whether you go to hell in the end because He is worthy."

It took me a while to understand what Paris Reidhead was talking about, because for years I thought we served Jesus to be nice people and get heaven in the end. What Paris Reidhead meant is, heaven has no worth without Jesus. "Would you still want to go to heaven if Jesus wasn't there?" is another way I've heard it put. In short, if you're not interested in having a drink with the Master, you shouldn't care much about the party.

Paris Reidhead said he'd rather go to hell and be with Jesus than go to heaven and be without Him. I realize that's impossible but at least I understand now what Paris was talking about. After you've lived a while, and seen trial and hurt, and after you've seen God provide year after year, victory and loss after victory and loss, you don't care much about mansions in Glory. You care about the Master in Glory. You don't care much about riding rainbows or raindrops, or any other pop-culture cliché about heaven. You care about Jesus, and about God, and about the Spirit, and you care about Their presence. Eventually, you come to a place in life where you say, I don't care where I end up in the end, I just want to be where You are. I'll go to any party, as long as You are with me.

---

I've always thought of Jesus as the description of the indescribable God, the definition of the undefinable. Some people say Jesus is the simplest form of God or that He's God understandable, made tangible. I like the thought of that, but even still Jesus has never been tangible to me. I have never seen Him, touched Him, heard His voice. But somehow I love Him, and I know Him still the same.

It's strange really, having such affection for a man who lived thousands of years ago, but it's true. The reason I want to go to heaven is because God is there, and Jesus is there, and the Holy Spirit is there. I don't care much about a big house or a street made of gold or wings or riding raindrops. I want to know God, I want to look into the face of Jesus, I want to feel the Spirit unhindered. Where They are is where I want to be, and if it's called Heaven, great.

## 43: the ebenezer

I once spent a weekend in Nashville at a songwriter's conference. For two days, I was surrounded by independent Christian artists in a cool room littered with candles.

We were there to learn how to make money and become famous. No one in the room would have put it that way, but honestly, it's why we gathered. Trouble is, we were all under-discovered, and if I'm honest, all under-talented. We were a unique group, a hopeful crowd, a people working, trying to use our gifts to make something beautiful. God-honoring, even.

Everyone had demos and EP's and LP's and CD's and DVD's and business cards, contact cards, and birthday cards. So many folks, so many dreams. It was a wonderful weekend now that I think about it. I didn't show up with CD's though. I brought a backpack, a Bible, a journal, and a disposable camera.

Honestly, I was there for one reason—to hear Andrew Peterson speak. I had been a long-time fan and he was giving the keynote speech on Saturday night. All day Friday and Saturday I walked around looking at booths, picking up albums and putting them down, asking questions, saying things like, "Yeah, that's a great place to print your promo posters," and "No, I didn't bring any CD's, I'm just here to hear Andrew Peterson."

Finally Saturday night came. I showed up early and sat at the table closest to the front. Andrew Peterson was introduced as "a man who writes songs with the heart and honesty of Rich Mullins." He thought that was an overstatement, I thought it was fitting. I was biased though. Rich and Andrew are legends to me.

Andrew Peterson walked on stage and said, "I'm not a speech giver, I'm a writer, so I've written out everything I'd like to say and I'm going to read it." Then he proceeded to read for 30 minutes, rarely looking up from his page. I proceeded to rarely look up from my page in attempts to write down everything he said.

That night started a process in me I'll never forget. Andrew Peterson told me I should write more. He said life was worth writing about, worth noting, worth telling of. Andrew Peterson spoke of having such a love affair with words that whether they be lyrics or stories or journal entries he simply couldn't imagine life without them.

While he shared, I had a hard time breathing. It could have been my childhood asthma acting up, or maybe it was that for the first time in a while I was receiving fresh air and my lungs didn't know what to do with it. Andrew Peterson inspired me deeply that weekend. He told me God doesn't care about my songs. He said God doesn't care whether or not I sell records or have a fan base or get my music here or there. He said God cares about each day drawing us an inch closer to His heart, because an inch toward God is an epic journey.

One of my favorite songs ever written is the old hymn, "Come Thou Fount Of Every Blessing." It was originally a poem by Robert Robertson penned in 1758. In the second verse he writes, "Here I raise mine ebenezer, hither by Thy help I'm come, and I hope by Thy good pleasure, safely to arrive at home."

In college I went to Dr. Bob's office and asked him what an ebenezer was and he told me about 1st Samuel chapter 7 when Samuel took a stone and set it up to symbolize and remember, "The Lord has helped us." The stones were meant to remind. The ebenezer was a symbol of the substance, a picture pointing to the other picture, a helpful hint testifying of a God who helps.

If I would have had a rock that night in Nashville, I would have placed it somewhere and I would have thanked God for using Andrew Peterson to help me. Andrew's words sent me toward my words. God used a storyteller to provoke me to tell my story.

## 44: the second advent

When the couple in love, in the Garden of love, bit the fruit of un-love, a love previously unknown was revealed: a love that forgives. A love of discipline. A love of sacrifice. A love that responds to betrayal. In short, the love of God in full counsel.

I say it was not yet present but I don't mean it was not yet in motion. Somehow, in the mind of God, there was already a plan in response to this original sin. Jesus was not made up as a band-aid for Adam's folly. God did not grow anxious and bite His cosmic nails when the snake deceived. He didn't need to take a smoke break and think it over. God knew, and God only knows how He knew, but He knew. There was not and never will be a Plan B.

Plan A, though, is fascinating. It began with the man Abraham, and the people of Israel and continued to Moses and an exodus and to David the King and to Isaiah the Prophet and the tribe of Judah. The story made its way to a carpenter named Joseph and a virgin named Mary. And the script was set in a city you would be hard pressed to find on a map. So many people, so many small stories, all telling one story, all speaking of one Person. The entirety of the Law and the Old Testament, the foreshadowing, the prophecies, the longing of a people, the whole world waiting for a crescendo found in one word: advent.

This invisible God had a language about Him. A language hard to follow, hard to understand, because it seemed progressive, it seemed both ancient and new. And this language always seemed to point to an appearing, a development, a materialization of that which many believed impossible to materialize. God was going to one day make things right. His followers knew this, but the hope was met with confusion. For when God appeared, when the Virgin gave birth and Jesus breathed His first breath of humanity's air, it was in no palace, no place of power, there was no great ceremony. Rather the One who made the world was born in one of the worst places the world has to offer: the filthy, cold dirt of a stranger's barn.

God can do anything. He can speak oceans into being and speak oceans into parting and speak oceans into calming. But, from the outside, it seems He couldn't find a decent place for His Son to be born. Or, in God's view of the world, this place was perfect for the first advent. God does everything on purpose. He purposed, from before the world began a place to birth Jesus. God knew who Mary would be. He knew who Joseph would be. And He knew the cost of eating that fruit would be a debt only He Himself could pay.

So that pristine birth, on that un-pristine floor, by that nearly pristine woman, was humanity's first taste of perfection, and God's first taste of flesh and blood. Just as a director of a grand orchestra taps his podium to set the tempo of the music, so the Director of Heaven and Earth tapped His intro for His one and only Song. And this would be a song of longsuffering, so it needed to be set in a place worthy of the music and more importantly worthy of the Man singing the solo.

---

Jesus walked the world in perfect obedience. He was tempted in every way a first century man was tempted but He never caved. His resolve was unyielding, His passion connected to His purpose. At first glance you might think He's just a nice guy, a good Jewish man doing good Jewish things, but the more time you spend around Him the more you see the fire in His eyes. You sense He was not only leading but somehow being led. You're challenged and intrigued. You want to both walk away and draw near. There will never be a man more fascinating than Jesus.

His perfect life allowed Him to die a perfect death and do so in perfect obedience. That doesn't mean it was easy. It means quite the opposite really. I don't know if Jesus felt more than a normal person. I don't know if He had supernatural capacity, but I know He could look into a man's eyes and see his soul. And I can imagine, if you have the ability to see souls as well as people, if your depth of insight is deeper than most, then maybe, you carry the capacity to feel extraordinarily deep pain, or joy for that matter.

I once heard Matt Chandler say his favorite thing about Jesus was that no matter what you go through, no matter how bad it gets, you can never look at Jesus and say, "Jesus, You don't understand." If you look at Jesus and say, "I've been betrayed. I've been abused. I've been taken advantage of. My friend died. I feel alone. No one understands me," Jesus can look back at you and say with compassion, "I know." Sometimes I think God came to Earth for those words, "I know. Me too."

---

The first advent—or appearing—of Jesus was confusing because people wanted Him to overthrow the Roman Empire and reign as an earthly King. But Jesus knew that was too shortsighted. Therefore, His agenda and mission seemed counterintuitive. He flashed moments of strength but it always seemed He was holding back. He never spoke of schemes and battle plans. Jesus didn't own a sword. He didn't seek a throne. He had a humble self-confidence and assurance. He fought by healing—even His anger was an expression of love. To clear the temple and to curse the Pharisees was loving, we may not see it as such, but Jesus fluently spoke the language of God and God only knows one language— love.

The first arrival was the dawn of an era. The era of new creation. The era the first garden had broken and trampled. Jesus brought the story of a new garden, a story of two new gardens.

In the Garden of Gethsemane, Jesus suffered and pled with God and remained faithful. And in the Garden of Resurrection, Jesus conquered death and made right what had been wrong. We have the option of gardens. If we remain faithful in our suffering, in our Saturday, and if we plead well and stay true then we will be rewarded with resurrection. Death will have no sting and our wrongs will be made right. But we cannot have Resurrection without Gethsemane.

The second advent of Jesus will not be a different Jesus, but the same Jesus seen in different light. Second Advent Jesus will not be holding a scale or a clipboard. He'll have a sword and a mission. And this mission will not involve letting others take His life. This time, at this His second arrival, Jesus will have in His hands the matter of life and death. He will appear and He will bring division.

He will not seek justifications or explanations or conversations, for the time will have passed for that. He will want to know if we've been to Gethsemane. He will raise with Him those who've died with Him. We will be divided. It will be terrible or joyous. There is no middle ground with Second Advent Jesus. He's paid too much to leave margins. Peace came first—war will come second.

## 45: the rest of the story

It's been five years since my parents reconciled. They recently bought a house together. Well, kind of. My dad bought a house and my mom lives there. They have two dogs. I think my parents love each other again. At least kind of love each other. But I also think they are afraid and playing it safe.

There are moments when I believe in them, glimpses of moments when they laugh together, hold hands, go to movies. I tell my dad he needs to pursue my mom, speak tenderly to her, write letters, bake cookies, whatever it takes to win her heart. He's jaded though. He has trust issues. He's told me about it on more than one occasion. Before I met and married beautiful Amy, he was giving me speeches about women and how they can't be loyal and how marriage is a piece of paper and on and on he'd go. It made me sad for him.

As I've grown up and out of their house and now that I pay my own bills, our conversations are different, much more candid. I don't have to listen and agree anymore. I can honor my dad differently now, mostly by sharing a worldview that's not pessimistic and victimized. My dad is not a victim, and he's not hopeless, he's just hurt and tired, and he doesn't know how to respond. He's paralyzed by fear and frustration and he's wearing invisible handcuffs. Truth is, these feelings are natural, but when they live in a calloused heart they become deadly.

I remember the first real Gospel conversation I had with my dad. He picked me up in Houston after a mission trip I went on. It was raining so hard that night we had to pull under a covered carwash to transfer my bags from the church van to his truck. This mission trip was one of the first I'd ever helped lead. I was 20 and serving as a youth intern at a church in Southeast Texas. This particular mission trip was highly evangelistic.

Once we arrived at the church we were working with, we were put in teams of four and sent out all over the city doing surveys. We would knock on someone's door, tell them who we were, and if allowed, we'd ask a few questions. The final question on the survey was, "If you died right now, would you go to heaven or hell?"

I was 20 at the time so it took me 10 houses before I realized this question was foolish. Maybe I never would have realized if it wasn't for house number 10.

When we walked to the door I decided to stay back a bit and let the others in my group have a turn. We had a few awkward conversations with people prior to house number 10 but I was counting them as persecution for the sake of Christ. Little did I know they were self-inflicted persecutions that probably had little to do with Christ. Anyhow, my team consisted of four junior high students, and at house 10 they were going to lead the survey. We knocked on the door and I stepped back a few feet on the porch. I wanted to be close enough to hear but not close enough to be a part of the conversation.

A younger man opened the door. He looked a few years older than me but still young enough where I considered him a peer. He smiled when he saw the students at the door and welcomed our survey. The first few questions were breezed through without much worry. He spoke with gentleness and didn't seem annoyed that the junior high students were taking forever to write down his answers. Eventually we arrived at the final question and a 13-year-old girl on my team looked up from her clipboard and asked, in a 13-year-old girl voice, "If you were to die right now, would you go to heaven or hell?"

Once the question was out there living in the air I looked away. I didn't want to apply any added pressure. Or maybe I was afraid. Maybe I felt awkward for the guy. Either way, I turned my head and pretended to be busy. Then I heard, "What's your name?" No one responded so I looked up and the guy from house 10 was talking to me. "What's your name?" he said again. "Josh," I told him, "my name is Josh." "Josh, nice to meet you; I'm James." He spoke right over the heads of the students and kept his eyes fixed on me.

James said, "Josh, you seem like an alright guy, being out here with these teenagers and all, but do you really think it's a good idea to knock on someone's door, and ask them a few questions, only to eventually get to the real reason you're here, which is, if I'm going to heaven or hell? Don't you think you should ask my name, maybe shake my hand, before you ask about my eternity?"

I just stood there, holding a clipboard, feeling like the world was coming into focus for me. I think James was a follower of Jesus, because as he walked back into the house he bent down and looked at the girl who asked the question and said, "I'm sorry you had to ask me that; I'm sorry you're having to go through this neighborhood asking everyone that. I'll pray for you, and I'll ask God not to let you get discouraged or to discourage others." Then James touched her on the head, said "Goodbye, friends," and walked back into his house.

We walked away from house 10 and changed our first and final question. Instead of jumping right into the survey we started with, "Hello, what's your name," and we ended with, "We would love to pray for you and your family, is there anything that you'd be willing to let us pray with you about?"

The day went much better from there. Sometimes, after our new final question, the people at the door would bow their heads and close their eyes, assuming we were going to pray on the spot, so we'd jump to it, and ask God to meet their needs. These questions went a lot better for us. These questions brought about conversation and gentleness in the tone of the homeowners, not defensiveness.

When my dad picked me up in the covered carwash in Houston I had an unbearable weight on my heart. I knew I needed to tell him the story of Jesus very openly and boldly. I knew my dad had grace issues and father issues, and I knew it wasn't going to be easy, but I had to speak.

We went to eat at a fast food place and he asked me about the trip. I used the story of James to get into the conversation. I told my dad I felt foolish for leading four junior high students into such a tough situation. He listened quietly.

My dad has worked in the oil fields all his life. He did a stint of work on an oil-rig off the Gulf of Mexico that required a helicopter to take him to work. Other than that, all I've known him to do is wake up at 5:00 A.M., put on his work boots, head out into the muggy mosquito-infested miles of oil fields, work hard days, and at the end of the month get what he deserved.

There's no grace in the oil fields. One mistake can get you killed. These types of men function under one premise—we're out here to feed our family. There's no badge of honor in working with oil. Your hands are always dirty, your back always tired, and your phone always on. If a leak happens, you're called out; no matter the time, you're responsible to go fix the problem—because problems don't fix themselves. And again, the food on the table depends on it.

But grace doesn't live like that. Grace is undeserved. You can't wake up early and go out and get it. It comes to you, like a gift from an old friend, an old friend you betrayed long ago.

Introducing my dad to Old Friend Grace was like introducing an Eskimo to the stock market. It's not that he can't understand, it's that he has no context, no reference point. My dad has told me on more than one occasion that he believes he will get a fair shake with God, that in the end God will look at him and say, "Kyle, you're a hard worker, and I respect that; and you open doors for people, and that's really nice; and you're better than most people and you're not a racist; so, come on in, heaven is yours."

I've told my dad on more than one occasion that his fair shake with God is Jesus. I've told him the gift of grace is simply that—a gift. But it's not easy, sometimes it's hard to remember that the first time an Eskimo—even the smartest Eskimo—walks on Wall Street the world is foreign.

At the fast food restaurant in Houston, I told my dad—because of God's holiness, we have no chance to be right with Him. I told my dad Jesus was perfect and laid down His life in our place, so if we identify with His death as if it was ours, and if we identify with His resurrection as if it will be ours, and if we live in light of His sacrifice then God will be pleased with us and accept us into Himself. Heaven is ours, because heaven is Him.

I told my dad I wanted to spend eternity with him. I told him I wanted to be sure he knew the right story and I wanted to tell him, because I loved him, and love tells hard stories, because love is truth, and truth is hard.

I wish I could tell you my dad believed me that night. But, he didn't. He heard me though. And because of that conversation over the last 8 years I've been able to have many more. He's opened up to me about his upbringing. He told me he had to go to church when he was younger. His father made him go and he hated it. My dad thought everyone there was a hypocrite.

He told me about his mother, my grandmother, and how she was a closet alcoholic and how she battled cancer and how one night he had to carry her up a flight of stairs to her apartment because she was so weak.

My dad still goes to Granny's grave-site once a month to clean off the tombstone and rake the leaves and sit down and talk with her. His discipline is impressive.

My dad's heart is opening to Jesus. Slowly, sure, but progressing nonetheless. He's growing more intrigued and moved by Old Friend Grace. He's being drawn in and it's beautiful to watch. Our relationship is much more open now, and he's told me in honest moments he wishes he could be as convinced as I am of the unseen.

He's also lost his cynicism. One night on the back porch he was smoking a cigar talking to me and he said, "Josh, I want to take back all that stuff ,I used to say about marriage. When I saw you and Amy get married I thought to myself, they'll make it. Because you and Amy are the kind of people who won't give up on each other. You're not like me and your mother; you guys believe in the same things, and believing in the same things is more important than people realize."

The only way my parents will ever fully be made right is when they come to a place where they connect on a soul level. They are moving, I'm just not sure it's always in the right direction. It's difficult when you want to make someone believe something and it won't happen. I've never had a time in life where someone looked at me and said, "You're right, I'm going to become a follower of Jesus because your arguments are better than mine." So, I don't argue. I pray. I wait. I hope, that soon, the Light of the Son of Man will take away their fears and reveal to them the rest of the Story.

## 46: the Friday

When I was 8 years old I watched a movie about Jesus with my grand-mother.  She sat in her rocking chair crocheting a blanket and I laid on the couch.  When Jesus was nailed to the cross, I remember crying so heavily my grandmother had to put down her blanket and come sit by me and tell me it was just a movie.  I kept saying, "Why are those people be-ing so mean?  Jesus didn't do anything wrong."  My understanding was limited, sure, but injustice isn't hard to spot at any age.

My grandmother turned off the movie before the resurrection sce-ne.  I was washing my face and going to bed before she could tell me the rest of the story.  Or maybe she did, and I forgot.  Either way, I went to bed afraid.  I felt terribly empty.  The whole world seemed hopeless.  I held the covers to my chin, thinking about time and space and everything I'd learned in history class and how for years before us people have lived and for years after us people will live.

I paralyzed myself thinking far into the future.  Eventually I started crying again.  This was the tune of my life for a few years.  The tears came and went, but the haunting reality of death loomed over me.  I would look at pictures of relatives who'd died and feel empty.  I'd think, "They will never live again, ever.  How sad."

Someone eventually told me the nice guy from the movie came

back from the dead. Eventually the hole in my chest was filled with hope. The rest of the story helped ease the pain, but those first feelings of darkness were frozen in my memory, and they took years to melt away.

That was my first taste of Friday.

---

The day the Son of God was killed has gone by many names. The English called it Crucifixion Friday. The Germans called it Mourning Friday. To others it was Holy Friday, Black Friday, Great Friday, Good-Bye Friday, and to some—God's Friday. I think God's Friday is my favorite. Seems fitting—that everything would be God's, even the day His Son died.

I'm grateful to live on the other side of God's Friday because I'm not sure I could deal with the despair dealt that day. The made-for-tv movie was enough to break me. The real Friday would have crushed me, Saturday nothing would have paralyzed me, and resurrection Sunday...well.

The only place where God is absent is the grave. If you were to call roll in the graveyard, when you came to Jesus' name, someone in class who knew Him would have to speak up and say, "Jesus isn't here; He was here, but He left and never came back."

Sunday brings hope to Friday, just as Friday brings meaning to Sunday. God's Friday is irrelevant without God's Sunday, just as God's Sunday is irrelevant without God's Friday. Though God needs nothing, He chose to build the world in such a way that the empty tomb doesn't work without the cross, and the cross doesn't work without the empty tomb. They are not mutually exclusive. And that's Good News.

The prophet Isaiah—many years before the birth of Christ—wrote that God would crush the future Savior, and it would be His joy to do so. So, something the Christian must come to terms with is: God killed Jesus, and it was His joy to do so. But not only did God kill Jesus, Jesus was obedient to His Father, laid down His life, willingly endured the cross, and it was His joy to do so. God was behind the death of Jesus, but Jesus' life was not taken, it was given—the cross is a both and. The cross is God's demand met by God.

As much as God killed Jesus, so too, Jesus had Himself killed. And this, as Dr. Bob says, was agreed upon before the world began. I didn't understand this when I was younger, and even still I have a hard time getting my mind around it. God being behind the death of Jesus seems counterintuitive, and Jesus being behind the death of Jesus seems bizarre. But bizarre as it may be, it's the heartbeat of the Gospel, and the lifeblood of the Christian faith.

The death agreement between God and Jesus was in motion before the world began but it was surely signed in the Garden of Gethsemane. Right before Jesus' trial, we find Him alone praying, sweating drops of blood, overwhelmed to the point of death. Jesus is afraid. He's tired. He knows what's coming: within hours He'll bear on His shoulders the full weight of the wrath of God. But what's important, and so healing to realize, is that in this moment Jesus is not agonizing with fear of the Romans. He is not sweating blood because of cruel soldiers, nails, whips, and a crucifixion. The Son of God is tormented because He is being asked to drink fully the cup of God's wrath, a cup only He is qualified to drink.

He's being asked to be God forsaken.

Within hours, the eternal rescue mission will become actual—that the One who created the world would humble Himself, come to the world through a virgin birth, grew to become the sinless, miracle-working prophet, priest, king, carpenter from Nazareth; fully God and man, fully beaten, mocked, crucified and buried, all for the sins of the world, and all for the salvation of those who believe. The Jesus in the Garden helped pen the Story. And even though He was co-Author, what we find in the Garden is that the weight of it all is already killing Him.

The reason Martin Luther called the cross "The Great Exchange" is because what happened on God's Friday was a double imputation. It goes back to what R.C. Sproul was talking about. The sin of Adam and you and me was nailed to Jesus on the cross, and in exchange the righteousness of Jesus was gifted to us, imputed to us. The cross of Jesus is where justice and mercy kiss. The cross is both the only acceptable payment of sin and the only acceptable avenue to righteousness. And it has to be this way—for before a holy God our greatest merits are embarrassing and our résumés shameful.

But, when we trust in the imputed righteousness of Jesus, when we understand the only righteousness we have is because of Jesus, then we can stand before God as confidently as Jesus. If R.C. Sproul taught me anything it is this—the cross is just as much about righteousness as it is about forgiveness. And if we add anything to the cross for salvation, such as works or morality or merit of our own, we are outside of Biblical Christianity. Justification before God comes through the cross alone, not moral religion.

The glory of God's Friday is that both God and Jesus, by the power of the Holy Spirit, joyfully made the way for our reconciliation, forgiveness, and righteousness. The writer of the book of Hebrews even says about Jesus, "For the joy set before Him, He endured the cross, scorning its shame." It was His joy to make all things right with His Father. Christ on the cross is the ultimate good work. Therefore, every good work we do now, and every line of our résumé, is not to gain God's approval but rather because in the cross we have been given God's approval.

We should be motivated to works because we're no longer condemned but commended. To say it plainly—we don't work for righteousness—we work from righteousness. We do not work for approval—we work from approval. We do not go to the cross and plead our case—we go to the cross because it's where Jesus pleads our case. We do not go to the cross and demand we've earned something—we go to the cross because we could never earn anything. A crown of righteousness is given to us because a crown of thorns was given to Jesus. We deserved the thorns. We got the righteousness.

The exchange was greater than we will ever know.

The cross of God's Friday is our hope and glory. The cross is the only thing the believer is to boast in. For we know Sunday is coming, and we know the death of Jesus is not the end of the story. It is just the beginning.

## 47: the Saturday

The local church was meant to be a messy place—a unique gathering bent toward those who are not well. Rich Mullins once said he never understood people who didn't go to church because, as they say, "Too many hypocrites go to church."

Rich Mullins said he went to church to get help. He said he would tell anyone that. He believed by parking his car in the church parking lot he was showing anyone who drove by that he wasn't perfect. Rich Mullins believed everyone but pretenders should have a place in the church. He saw the local church as a place for the broken, unperfected ones, and he thought by attending, you were freely admitting to everyone present, "Yeah, me too."

I think our problem is, somewhere along the way we forgot "Yeah, me too" is not an agreement of personal perfection. It's the opposite. "Me too," in the context of the local church is, "me too, I'm being redeemed," "me too, I have doubts and fears and insecurities" and "yeah me too, I'm trying to overcome addiction" and "yeah me too, I'm working through that same sin." "Me too" is the anthem of a community in process—a tattoo on the soul of people daily walking away from who they use to be. "Me too" is the journey from the superficial into the authentic, from shallow to deep.

"Me too" is the feeling of normal.

---

A few years ago I attended a morality debate between an atheist-turned-pastor friend of mine, and a well-known pastor-turned-atheist. The setting was a dimly lit college classroom. I knew the room so I showed up early. I was surprised to find the space already filling up. I hurried down front and wished my pastor friend a quick good luck. I didn't really know what to wish a guy who was about to debate, but nonetheless I shook his hand, said good luck, then went and took my seat.

For over an hour my friend and the atheist went back and forth and on and on about which is a better basis for morality—the God of the Bible, or no god at all. It was entertaining enough and I thought my friend was doing well. He was much funnier than the other guy and looked like he slept better the night before.

At the end of the debate, the pastor-turned-atheist was given the last word. He took a deep breath, gathered his notes, then tiredly looked out at the 500 or so people packed in the room, and said, "I'd like to close by quoting Jesus, out of Mark's Gospel chapter 2 where He says, "It is not the healthy who need a doctor, but the sick, for I have not come for the righteous but the sinner." Then he paused, exhaled, put his hands out and stated plainly, "If you are sick, and find yourself to be a sinner, then you have need for Jesus, and if not, then you don't. I find myself not to be sick and not to be a sinner, therefore I have no need."

I couldn't believe what he said. I moved to the edge of my seat and looked around the room. I wanted my pastor friend to walk up to the microphone and say, "He's right. If you go to Jesus with your sickness and sin, He'll receive you. He'll heal you in this life or the next, and He will give you right standing with the God who created the world."

I wanted someone to finish the story. I wanted to tell everyone in the room Jesus could be trusted. I walked to my car praying for those in attendance who had never gone to Jesus. I prayed because something in me believed Jesus was going to rescue people that night. I prayed because I think the odds are there are very few people in the world who really believe they are well and all is well. I'm not even sure if the atheist debater believed it. I think most people, if they are honest, or if life has pressed them long enough, will openly admit they are not as well as they put off.

I remember laughing as I drove home. I found the final words surreal and ironic on the part of the pastor-turned-atheist. Telling a crowd of college students they should go to Jesus to heal their sickness and sin is no way to win a debate.

---

Let's face it: we are not well, and we will stay not well this side of the second coming. So why pretend? Why be imprisoned by false perfection? Why ignore reality and secretly live miserable? And why be painfully unwilling to talk about it? Many of us are dying for a moment of "me too," but we'll die before we say it. Many of us need to feel normal, and desperately need someone to look into our eyes and say, "How are you really doing?"

Many of us are following Jesus the best we know how but are paralyzed by the fear and frustration of the meantime, and instead of calling our closest friends over, starting a pot of coffee, and being painfully honest about our struggles, we respond in the opposite way and live an internally miserable life of managing morality and manufacturing smiles. We become what we hate. We lose our minds. We lose our desire for community. We lose our love for Jesus. And worst of all we lose heart in the midst of the waiting. We fall away, and we don't have to.

Maybe it's because we do not know how to wait. Maybe we could learn something from those first followers of Jesus who sat together for that miserable day and a half. Often I think about that Saturday and the people who lived it. I wonder what it must have been like to know

Jesus, to have spent meaningful time with Him, to have known His laugh. And I often wonder how those who experienced the despair of Friday found strength on Saturday.

I like to think in the waiting those first followers told stories about Jesus. I like to think they remembered well, painfully well. I like to think they cried and they doubted and they hugged and at times said very little—because deep community is not afraid of silence.

But I also think they laughed, and they said to each other, "Remember the time Jesus did..." And I think they prayed, really prayed, and they trusted, really trusted, and they put all their hope in the truth that their friend Jesus was everything He said He was.

They gathered. They told stories. They waited. They bet their life on a Person. Maybe we could do the same. In this lifelong season of waiting for the appearing, what if we gathered, gave, prayed, trusted, and remembered.

What if we dreamed of the glory to come but were still dreadfully honest about today's tragedies. What if we ached for what had been lost and hoped of the justice and restitution to come. And what if we spoke truth to each other, listened to each other, and said to each other, "This is who I am, this is what God is doing in me, and this is what I'm dealing with. I need help. Can you help me?" And what if it worked. What if somehow the Spirit of God filled this process with His nearness and we were healed, preserved, purified. What if Jesus' brother James was right when he wrote, "Confess your sins to one another and you will be healed"? What if we realized Saturday nothing was the space where the Spirit was most able to meet us in our ache?

In the midst of our waiting, in the middle of our story, may we be so fortunate to have the Son of God appear. And may we, by the grace of God, be able to confess His Name in our midst, and be so discerning to recognize Him in our Saturday—for on the Sunday to come, there will be no doubt of who He is.

## 48: the Sunday

In rare moments, those with ears to hear can hear the other headphone.
In fleeting instances, one who senses can sense Sunday. But the moments
are rare and fleeting because this world's capacity for eternity is small.
Selfishness spoils Sunday's Song. And selfishness is our native tongue.
The language of now doesn't translate well to the language of forever.
There is a place though, where Resurrection reigns and everyone speaks
and understands. A place where no hospitals, hostels, orphanages, courtrooms, prisons, or prejudice exist—a place where the sun needs not shine
and the only thing absent is death.

Though it's available now, and Jesus prays we'd live it now, the
"Earth as it is in Heaven" promise can sometimes feel like fighting fog.
It's hard to believe you can win when the fog keeps moving and disap-
pearing and refuses to show more than glimpses of tangible touch. Clinging to the moments of Sunday, though, is the foundation of Saturday.
Fighting fog, as hard as it may be, is worth the effort. Or, as I've heard it
said, "The 'not yet' is worth the wait."

On "Earth as it is in Heaven" was meant to be more than a hope.
It's a prayer revealing to us the heart of Jesus and the love of God. When
someone identifies with the great exchange of God's Friday, then aligns
himself or herself with the church on Saturday, the nearness of eternal

Sunday's air becomes breathable. Sunday is both here now and there then.

Sunday is the other headphone.

---

The three most profound and provocative words in human history are—He is risen. The truth of those scandalous three words fueled our world's most monumental movement—because those words declare victory, and they have the audacity to say death's not the end.

One spring break in college I went to Mexico on a mission trip. We were going to partner with a local church in Nuevo Laredo. Two weeks prior they had moved into a building and needed help renovating.

The leader of our trip had a long-standing relationship with the pastor of the church we were going to work with. Our leader's name was Allan. He had been to Mexico many times and loved pastor Jamie and his family and his church. Allan had pictures of Jamie's children in his office. These men were brothers. On the day of the trip, we gathered to load into the 15-passenger vans and Allan told us horrible news.

The week before our trip, Pastor Jamie's wife and mother were killed in a car accident on their way to church. They were hit by a truck and killed instantly; it was the morning of the first service in the new building. Allan told the story through tears. He could hardly finish it, actually. Allan said he spoke briefly to Pastor Jamie and Jamie assured him we were still welcomed to come for the week. We said a prayer for Jamie and his family, then somberly loaded the vans.

The drive to Nuevo Laredo took about eight hours. Once we arrived Pastor Jamie was to meet us in the city and take us to the property. We left early enough to arrive in Mexico by the afternoon. As we wound through the city, filled with markets and traffic, Allan told us to look for a man wearing a blue shirt and a baseball hat. I was sitting in the closest seat to the front, in the middle, the front passenger seat open for Pastor

Jamie. As we neared the pick up spot, Allan reminded us of Jamie's loss and he encouraged us to be respectful.

Just as Allan finished talking we rounded a curve and saw a man in a blue shirt and baseball hat waving. It was Jamie. He started waving with both hands and walking into the middle of the road. He waited until we drove right in front of him, then joyfully drummed on the hood of the van and came and got in the front seat. Allan and Jamie embraced and after a few seconds I heard Allan say, "I'm sorry. Jamie, I'm so sorry." In a 15-passenger van full of college students, in the streets of Nuevo Laredo, two grown men held each other and cried. None of us said a word.

Eventually we heard horns honking and people telling us to move on, so we did. Allan and Jamie caught up as we drove. Jamie smiled and laughed and talked about the church and his children, and the work that needed to be done. He said he wasn't going to be able to work with us that day because he had arrangements to make regarding his wife and his mother but he would take us to a place where we would drop him off and then get directions for the last few miles.

We arrived in Mexico on a Saturday, the day before Easter Sunday. I remember this because when we dropped off Jamie at his appointment he and Allan hugged again, and before he got out of the van, Jamie turned to us and said with an accent full of peace, "Last week I buried my wife and my mother. It was the most painful thing I've ever done. But it has come at a hopeful time. For tomorrow is Easter, and if I've ever needed to know something, I need to know He is risen, and so we will be too."

Pastor Jamie was in a despair none of us had ever known, but he preached that Sunday with a brokenness and boldness I'd never seen before. For him, the resurrection of Jesus was real, and it affected the way he lived and moved and breathed. It affected his view of death and life. Sunday was more than Jamie's confession—it was his worldview. And a worldview lived under the banner of "He is risen" brings light to the darkest darkness.

## 49: the involved prayers

I still work in the church we started in Pullman, Washington. Honestly, it's hard. People are the business and people are difficult. And God is the business and He's no easier. For the first few years of our church I'd sit in coffee shops with large windows and watch people pass, wondering if what we were doing was making any difference. I'd try to pray and find my tongue broken.

After Amy and I were married and moved into our first place together, I found a bunch of old journals from high school. I looked through them and it was like I was reading words from someone who lived in another place and time; someone who knew a different Jesus than me. This previous person was involved, passionate, bold. He wrote out prayers the mature might call naïve. He was gutsy.

There was a time when previous version of me memorized two Bible verses a day. He also journaled daily for five months straight at one point. Younger me rolled out of bed onto his knees in prayer. Younger me cleaned out his closet and filled the walls with maps of the world and spent hours in there praying, placing his hand on each country asking God to save. Younger me had a discipline older me knows nothing of.

As I flipped pages and remembered what God brought me through, I reminded myself times have changed; I'm older now, busier,

195

more responsibilities to juggle; that was then, now's now. Even as the rationale spilled through my thoughts I heard younger me whisper, "But don't you miss it?"

I still pray, but it's not like I used to. Now I've developed a theology and a stance on God's stance toward this and that and now prayer is not so much about being involved with God as it is about me confirming my position. It's terrible really. I used to love God, but now, at times, it feels like I love knowledge about God. Knowing about God and knowing God are two different things. One causes your chest to puff out and the other causes your chest to cave in. I remember Dane would say, "If everything you learn doesn't send you back to your knees in worship than you've learned for nothing."

Recently I read about an old Jewish tradition where young boys studying the Torah for the very first time were given a drop of honey after they read their first line. Can you picture it, a child reading the holy words of an ancient God, then tasting honey. Surely he went back to his seat thinking, "I want more."

Teachers wanted these young men to associate study and prayer with the sweetness of honey. They wanted to teach that God is worth knowing, and knowing Him is sweet. So many times I read in the New Testament interactions Jesus had with the Pharisees and Teachers of the Law, and it feels like He's saying, "You've tasted the honey, but how soon you forget." In John chapter 5, I wonder if the light came on for the first time for any of those men. I wonder if any of them re-tasted the honey.

I think younger me read and prayed and drank his fill of honey. In the first years of our church, older me lost his love for the comb. I was tired all the time, stressed all the time, and my heart grew cold as my body went through the motions.

One of the reasons I think we don't pray is because we don't realize what's at stake. We can't physically see the opposition—we can't hear the enemy drawing near—we are an arm's length from suffering and trial.

I remember on the first Sunday after September 11th, 2001, our church was so packed we had to pull out extra seats. During the service our pastor asked the congregation to get on their knees for prayer, and once we all knelt he joined us and said, "Lord we're on our knees, because you've knocked us to them."

Sometimes you have to kneel or lie on your face before you can really feel the weight of your smallness. Sometimes you have to take a posture of helplessness to feel your helplessness.

Truth is, when trial comes our prayers change—they become far more aggressive. Pain speaks loudly—the unexpected sends us to our knees. If we knew what was coming after our homes and marriages and churches I think we would find ourselves on our knees more, on our face more, crying out, "Intervene, please, God; get involved."

The point of prayer is not answers; it's involvement. Karl Barth wrote, "To clasp the hands in prayer is the beginning of an uprising against the disorder of the world." Prayer is counter-human and counter-world. It's calling for uprising. It's engaging with a God capable of doing the impossible.

Prayer is about perspective, alignment, relationship, vision, and movement—it's about getting into the story of what God is doing and being bold enough to ask for more. When we pray well, we abide well.

Amy and I have prayed for our friends who are having trouble paying the bills or for our friends who are trying to get pregnant and when we were finished, looked at each other and said, I'm sorry for being selfish today, or for earlier when I was short with you. Prayer pulls the picture into focus, it brings the wayward heart home.

I have a friend named Nick who believes his prayers change things. I love praying with Nick because he talks to God like he knows Him, like they're old friends or something. Over lunch one day, Nick told me for ten years he's volunteered with a ministry called The Healing Room. Nick said through that ministry and in his personal life he's prayed for thousands of sick people. Only once has he seen someone healed.

I asked him about it, and he was reluctant to share. Eventually, between bites, he said, "Three years ago, a blind man was healed." I listened in silence, and as Nick shared, I believed him, because he never shifted his eyes. He spoke with humility, and he gave credit to God. Nick said God was very gracious to let him be involved.

Nick leads our church staff in prayer every Monday. A couple weeks ago he and his wife Tammy sat on a couch next to each other holding hands, teaching us how prayer works in their family. They said they take prayer seriously, and only tell people they can pray for them if they really have time to pray for them. Toward the end of the meeting, Nick and Tammy told our staff, "We just don't want to get to the end of our lives and have God tell us, "You didn't ask for enough. I would have done so much more if you would have asked."

---

A.W. Tozer said, "The most important thing about a person is what they think of when they think of God." If you think God's angry all the time you will pray and live accordingly. If you think God helps those who help themselves, again, you'll live according. There are some people who think God knows everything so why pray at all, and others who think prayer was invented so God can give us material stuff. But there are others still, who with pure hearts, daily get on their knees and faces before God making their gratitude and petitions known, and God, like a loving Father, answers them, and involves Himself with them. And these people are better for it, they're involved.

## 50: the unresolved

For the last four years I've only seen my parents on holidays and special occasions. In a good year I'll see them three times. I can get depressed if I let myself think about it. I love my family. It's not easy being away.

What's more depressing is when I go home I can feel the distance spanning across the kitchen table into our hearts. The conversations don't pick up as fast as they used to. The shallow end of the pool is where we swim if we're not careful. Relationships are hard, God knows, making things meaningful takes work. You don't accidentally get to the truth of it.

My mom is addiction-free as far as drugs go, but her addictive personality has found new outlets. She was making jewelry for a while, hundreds and hundreds of pieces of jewelry. Recently she's into making decorative crosses and she still enjoys a good puzzle. Last time I was home I helped her put a puzzle together. I only found where two pieces go. But I sat with her, and it was wonderful.

In the last two years my mom has rearranged the house a hundred times, painted the walls and put up pictures, took them down, hung them again. The three-car garage out back is filled with my mother's projects.

Finding work isn't easy for someone with a felony. And finding self-confidence is nearly impossible. The last time my mother and I talked

I saw new lines on her face, new need in her eyes. She told me she was lonely, tired, dying for purpose. She pours herself out on her kids and her dogs and her art, but even still she's longing for a deeper sense of community and worth. She needs—as we all do—the comfort of an eternal God and grace of the local church. She needs someone to ask how she's really doing.

The song being sung in my parents' new home is cordial enough, but if they listened they'd hear a distant voice whispering, "Better is available." Last week I asked my dad if he had plans to marry my mom again. He said things were great the way they were. He's fine with the current song. I think he's still scared. He's comfortable and still scared.

My dad doesn't realize God built women for commitment—nurture and nurturing—shelter and security. My dad won't submit to the truth that a woman who feels unloved and uncommitted to can't find her feet on solid ground. My mother is that woman and she's in free fall, wondering where the ground is. My dad doesn't realize God still has a plan for him and my mom. My dad thinks the game is in overtime when truth is they're at halftime. He doesn't realize he's the leader.

I told my dad it's not right the way they live. I've told him his experience of marriage doesn't blemish God's purpose for marriage. You don't walk out of a bad movie thinking every movie ever made is bad, and you don't hear a bad song and hate music wholesale. But I guess those rules don't apply when you walk out of a bad marriage.

The art of second chance is overrated in my dad's mind. He thinks he's doing right by providing a house, providing money. I've told him a house is simple and foundational and nothing heroic. What God finds heroic is a man laying down his pride and loving his wife and family over and over again until the end. But it's "forgive, don't forget" in their relationship. It's like what they had before was war, and now my dad's a wounded vet and my mom is a betraying ex-lover to keep close but not too close. It's sad really, but what is sadder still is the distance and insecurity that lives in that house.

---

Andrew Peterson has a song called "Dancing In The Minefields." In the tune he sings about him and his wife getting married young, buying their rings at a pawnshop, and committing to each other against all odds. Andrew Peterson says marriage is like dancing in a minefield or sailing in a storm.

The song came on the radio last month as Amy and I drove to the airport to catch a flight to Houston. It was five in the morning; the bold glow of a faint orange sun in the distance was slowly crawling over the snow-laced Eastern Washington Hills. It was the Palouse at its finest.

In the second verse Andrew Peterson sings, "'I do' are the two most famous last words, the beginning of the end, but to lose your life for another I've heard, is a good place to begin. 'Cause the only way to find your life, is to lay your own life down, and I believe it's an easy price, for the life we have found. So let's go dancing in the minefields, sailing in the storm, this is harder than we dreamed, but I believe that's what the promise is for."

He goes on to say, "We bear the light of the Son of Man, so there's nothing left to fear, so, I'll walk with you in the shadowlands till the shadows disappear, 'cause He promised not to leave us, and His promises are true, so, in the midst of all this chaos, baby, I can dance with you."

Amy was asleep in the passenger seat that morning. Still I reached over and grabbed her hand during the song, and I told her I loved her. And I prayed for my parents. I asked God to get involved in their lives, to break their hearts for one another. I asked God to give my parents eyes to see their need for Him. I asked Jesus to restore like He's done so many times. I asked God to bring resolve.

---

Much of life will never resolve. I have a cousin, Jay, who died when he was 16 years old. No one knows what happened. Some doctors said it was a brain aneurism, some said I'm sorry we don't know.

Jay's death paralyzed a lot of people in my family. He was the youngest of eight grandkids. People couldn't believe God would allow this. My uncle went to the gravesite every night for the first month after Jay's death, drinking beer and saying he was sorry. My aunt claims Jay is behind little things that happen throughout the day. If a door's left open, my aunt will say, "Hey, Jay, that's funny. Why are you messing with me today?" My grandmother cries if you mention his name. My grandfather's silence told his story.

My cousin Jay was a good kid. He grew up in a rough environment; his parents loved him, but they were struggling to make ends meet for years. And his father was in and out of jail more times than I could keep up with. Jay was special, he had a tender heart and he wasn't interested in drinking beer and smoking pot. He loved our grandparents. Everyday after school he'd stop by our grandparents' house and help our grandpa with projects and let our grandma feed him tacos. He wasn't rebellious. He was gentle and kind. He would look you in the eyes when you spoke to him.

Eight months before Jay died, I had a concert at a local church in their town. Jay came, as did much of my family. After the show Jay got connected with the youth minister in the church who was a friend of mine. Jay took to church like most kids take to video games. He got involved and started serving immediately. Within two months he had publicly confessed his love for Jesus and was baptized.

Grief is a weird thing. We talk to the deceased, we stay up late and stare at the ceiling, we make car decals and tee shirts and get tattoos. We want to find hope, but it's not easy. Unexpected death carries hopelessness like a disease. We will do anything to make ourselves feel better. In the wake of tragedy, even the strongest have the desire to medicate.

The unresolved must have answers; the Saturday is too dark to stare at. Something has to bring peace. But sometimes, it doesn't feel as though God is enough. We forget answers are dead.

---

My grandmother asked me to speak at my grandfather's funeral. On the flight down I typed out everything I wanted to say. I wrote words filled with hope and healing. I thought I would inspire everyone—tell them death shouldn't hurt or sting.

At the viewing, we all wrote letters to my grandfather and placed them in his casket as our final goodbye. As I wrote my letter, I told my grandfather I was jealous of him. I was at a funeral with my family, writing a letter, experiencing the ache of loss, while he was at a wedding with Jesus, experiencing the glory of Sunday. I told my grandfather to save me a seat at the party and to go ahead and fill my wine glass.

When we got to the cemetery and I looked down at my grandfather's headstone next to my cousin Jay's, I didn't feel like giving inspiration. I again felt a deep, aching sense of jealousy. So, I told everyone, "My name is Joshua, I'm the oldest grandson of Adolfo Lara, and I'm hurting. But I'm not hurting just because of loss, I'm hurting because there's a reunion happening, and I long to be a part of it."

I told everyone I pictured a wedding—but not a wedding of earthly relationships—a wedding of a great King and a great Bride. I told them I was jealous of Grandpa and Jay because they had seats at an eternal table. Grandpa and Jay were seeing clearly what we see through stained glass. They were hearing fully what we hear through one headphone. I told everyone I longed to be there too, dancing to the music.

I told them every funeral of an adopted saint should be grieved in light of the Great Wedding of the Greatly Redeemed. Every tear should be filled with sorrow and joy—every heart bursting with contentment and ache—every soul overwhelmed with fatigue and expectancy.

The promise of the future city of God should poise us to wait well, knowing one day the suffering will cease, the promise will come, the darkness will die. This doesn't mean knowing God makes things easy. It means knowing God makes things bearable. It means at some point—be assured—our free fall will find foundation.

I hope my parents remarry. I really do. I hope our world sees the Light of the Gospel of Jesus and we tell the Story well. I hope we live understanding Saturday Nothing is fleeting; it's merely a doorway, a prelude to the prelude, a momentary mix of trouble and joy preparing us for Sunday—glorious Sunday—the Day of the Wedding, the Day when all things will be made right.

You may feel like you're stumbling through the dark for an eternity of nothing, but take heart, don't lose hope, soon enough night will surrender to day, and Saturday Nothing will become Sunday Everything.

## A Word Of Thanks

It took a while to write these words. I think it's because for a while I didn't know what I was writing. I'd sit down and type, but I wasn't sure where I was going or who was leading.

I knew I wanted to tell my story, but I never created a story line—hence the lack of linearity. I hope you didn't mind too much.

Honestly, I didn't think I could write a book. I thought you needed permission or something. For almost a year, I figured I was wasting my time. I thought no one would want to read this.

But, I kept typing. And, after many mornings and many words, the story started to tell itself. It wasn't easy, it wasn't always where I thought we'd go, but as I kept working, the trail of crumbs kept leading.

Eventually, I finished. After three years of writing and re-writing I was ready to move forward. I filmed a Kickstarter video to raise money for publishing and posted it online. My goal was to raise the money in 40 days.

The total cost was raised in eight hours.

That was an overwhelming Thursday.

If you're reading these words you're probably one of those people who supported me. I'm so humbled to call you a friend, and so thankful you willingly gave to this work. You made these pages possible, and it's been a joy to share this story with you.

I'll never forget what happened with this book, and with my friends. You have given me a lifetime story, one that I'll tell when I'm Ronald Reagan's age, and for that I'm grateful.

## Kickstarter Supporters

Without these fine folks, Saturday Nothing would have never made it to print. So, to the following incredibly generous people who made this possible, I raise my glass of thanks.

Lance and Jennifer Logue
Aaron and Jenny Phillips
Adam and Kendall Conley
Brandon and Megan Williams
Haydn and Sarah Roberts
Josh and Andrea Broughton
Don and Lynda Rush
Brian Newman
Raquel Gamez
Drew Worsham
Jay Price
Connor and Kristin Wittman
Josh and Jamie Smart
Leslie Mullino
Gary Lau
Ron and Nancy Vanlandingham
Jason and Tara Taylor
Monroe and Rebekah Roberts
Sheri Fausett
Aaron Alford
Jesse and Caroline Rea
David and Leanne Smith
Austin Irby

Chad and Star McMillan
Danielle Oslager
Patti Pustka
Tyler and Krista Clayton
Siobhan Gallagher
Kat Swick
Jason and Darla Elder
Jeff Martin
Jennica Martin
Brent and Denise Fontenot
Jaclynn Gossett
Carol and Cleo Martin
Arlene Parkay
Rori Shaw
Mike Reinhardt
Rachel Walker
Matt and Laura Slotemaker
Nathan Quiring
Stephen and Whitney Petretto
John and Kati Weirick
Evan Blanshan
Tawni Foat
Ben Nelson
Ethan Johnson
Michael and Meredith Miller
Jordan and Christine Browning
Brandon and Sarah Strozier
Tommy and Carla Fajkus
Tannis Bogart
John and Michele Bender
Trent Nobles
Beth Van Wie
Jenica Tolleson

Burke Dagle

Megan Gerseny

Cameron Crabtree

Keith and Paige Wieser

David Bender

Will Hughes

Mattea York

Phil and Lou Walleck

Katrina Harris

Heather Weitman

John and Suzy Sypert

Jake Cheek

Kate Lynne Logan

Erika Ottenbreit

Sam and Kerri Thornton

Eric Foss

Pat and Melanie Gillen

Preston Dabbs

Branden Harvey

Cara Wade

Lauren Lengl

Jonathan Engel

Ron and Paula Sloot

Alli Furtado

Beckie Bruhn

Shaun Deffe

Hannah Porter

Daniel and Jessica Stancil

Stephen Shelton

Megan Thompson

Jen Smith

Susan Smethers

Sadie Porter

Jordan and Sami Elder

Becca Taylor

Alexis Weber

Emily Kutz

Ruth Hagel

Christy Stephens

Cheryl Rajcich

Jared Phares

Jamie Boyd

Amanda LaPlante

Suzzanna Lute

Kimberly Klein

Andrew Tweet

Cameron Flaming

Jacob and Jessica Dahl

Brian Kalwat

Luke Lengl

Kyle and Kacee Jackson

Matthew Hyndman

Amanda Brenna

Kori Jurgena

Kyle Spangenberg

Erin Dammon

Ryan and Harmony Davis

Megan McManus

Michael Rourke

Kylan Frost

RaeAnn Williams

Casey Fountain

Tommy Russell

Colleen Heckman

Brad Bartlett

Heather Hagen

Mark Crabtree

Tessa Hartman

Lauren Hodges

Rae Gremillion

Bob and Stephanie Nelson

Alexys Garcia

Pete and Jill Chambers

Jonathan and Erin Kidwell

Charlie and Lyndsey Robinson

Johnie Mays

Zanna Schultz

Christine Parks

Carly Cates

Andy Pollock

Wil McFarland

Craig Lovelace

Caleb Snoberger

Cory and Alayna Howell

Kade Melancon

Benjamin Bolshaw

David Hilts

Kate Stark

Paula Watson

Dorothy Worden

Zach Corcoran

Chelsey Rush

Bridget Wos

Charles Westerman

Victoria Lock

Tyler Weinbrecht

Darrell Halk

Abigail Tjaden

Beth Graham

Amanda Jen
Grant Godfrey
Jonathan Farwell
Michael Mishoe
Bradley Edge
Sarah Thompson
Nicole LeBlond
Anna Swanson
Michelle Goertzen
Kim Honeycutt
Joe and Bethany Larios
Nicole Erhardt
Anja Sundali
Coby Wilbanks
Chris and Lena Voth
Mark Rose
Colin Luoma
Ellie Frame
Scott Economu
Michelle Hall
Shivonne Hanks
Lori Browning
Connor Pomeroy
Allison Wilburn
Katie Eylander
Alyson Holder
Brandy Vaux
Lindsey Nichols
Matthew and April Young
Leighann Bottemiller
Amber Sirk
Kyle Florek
Joshua Gilman

Sarah Moore

Lindsay Graves

Steven and Britney Ayers

Connie Edmondson

Cherish Sharp

Lacey Rachal

Molly Boers

Jordan and Rebecca Nelson

Amanda Downen

Austin Storm

CPSIA information can be obtained at www.ICGtesting.com
Printed in the USA
BVOW032112151012

302851BV00002BA/1/P